WHAT PEOPLE ARE SAYING ABOUT *ENOUGH: A GOD WHO MEETS YOU WHERE YOU ARE*

Enough! Wow! What a tremendous revelation my friend Lafe Angell has written about so clearly in the pages of this book. From deep personal experiences he shares with you, the reader, to the treasures that burst forth on the pages of scripture, we clearly see that the God we serve, the God who has revealed Himself throughout the pages of scripture, is simply more than ENOUGH. This book is sure to enlighten you, encourage you, and invite you into a "more than enough" moment—a moment of a heavenly encounter with humanity's living Savior. Enjoy your time discovering what you may not have known or simply has never been revealed to you in a personal way, that He is more than ENOUGH!

~Bernie Moore • President, Bernie Moore
Ministries International • Evangelist

I was blessed to have gotten to know Lafe right before he and his wife, Hope, planted Grace Point and we became great friends instantly. You will find his story is inspiring and motivating and it teaches us that God not only has a plan but is able to accomplish those very plans through us. Remember as you're reading that what God has done for Lafe and Hope, He can do for you!

~Chris Binion • Founding & Lead Pastor,
Encounter Church, Fate TX

Pastor Lafe, in writing this book, captures the essence of sitting at a table and having a conversation. His practical insights and consistent down-to-earth examples will appeal to everyone. He uses his own experiences with biblical truths to enlighten the reader that God is indeed more than ENOUGH. If you find yourself in a season of uncertainty, this book is for you. If you are in a season and you are certain about God and life, this book is STILL for you.

~JAMES HUTCHINS • Author & Senior Pastor,
New Life Community Church, Frisco TX

If you want to deepen your relationship with God and truly find yourself in the process, this book will help you get there and with some laughs along the way! Through stories of laughter, pain, and even injury, Pastor Lafe shows each of us how simple it is to follow Christ. *Enough: A God Who Meets You Where You Are* will open your eyes to see that there is more to living this life with Christ as the center than just a boring confession of faith. It is an act that you live daily with God standing beside you through every moment. It is a journey of peace, joy, and laughter that not only changes your life but the lives of those around you.

~TIARRA TOMPKINS • Author • Literary Advisor • Writer • Editor

Lafe Angell is one of the most genuine and caring individuals I've ever met. The consummate encourager and servant leader, Lafe is the epitome of living life as a touchpoint of God's Grace in his local community. His dedication, commitment, and exemplary lifestyle inspires me at the highest level. His words and wisdom in this book will do the same for you.

~JOEL SCRIVNER • Lead Pastor, Oaks Church, McKinney TX

ENOUGH

ENOUGH

A God Who Meets You Where You Are

Lafe Angell

Carpenter's Son Publishing

Published by Carpenter's Son Publishing, Franklin, Tennessee
www.carpenterssonpublishing.com

Content Edit and Cover Design by Tiarra Tompkins

Edited by Ann Tatlock

Cover and Interior Design by Suzanne Lawing

Printed in the United States of America

ISBN: 978-1-956370-13-3 (print)

To my bride and my three gifts from heaven,
Callie, Caleb, and Noelle,
I love you so much more than I could ever possibly say.

To my Grace Point Family Church family,
You are an absolute gift and one of my greatest joys
is the honor of being your pastor. I so love y'all!

To you, dear reader,
I'm asking God to make this message come so alive
in your heart that you will experience the true joy
and the greatest adventure imaginable chasing after
God's heart and making it real in EVERY area of your life.

ACKNOWLEDGEMENTS

There is so much to be grateful for as this project has moved from a word from God that sustained me through a hard season of my life to a single message about His goodness I prepared for our church family, to a message series where there always seemed to be so much more to say that went a full 20 weeks!

That original word from God transformed my understanding of how to fully trust and walk with Him, and I knew I had to share it. I had been in a season where I felt completely insufficient to launch out and plant a church, but I knew that's what God had in mind. I wrestled with feeling and how to walk out this new thing God was bringing me to but like that original word from Luke 9, I heard a whisper in my heart. "Will you trust me with what is in your hands? I know you don't feel like you're enough, but I can do something big with your little."

At the end of the series a few people asked when it would become a book. My answer was that being a published author had never been a desire I felt the need to pursue. Then Liz, Kaycee, Sherri, and Marian got together to convince me that if I believed God put the message on my heart and kept speaking more and deeper with each passing week, I shouldn't just let it pass but should capture it for whoever God would speak to through it. If you picked up this book, that's you!

Liz Abbott, Kaycee Buckley, and Sherri Green (Sherri also goes by "Mom" and happens to be the greatest mother ever!)

Your work in helping to compile 142 pages of typed notes, with probably twice that number of transcript pages, was absolutely amazing! Your excitement and energy helped make the mountain manageable.

Marian Hays, your guidance and direction in the earliest stages of this book laid the foundation for what it became. Your insight as a published author in your own right was priceless in helping me process the steps necessary to go from concept to completion.

Tiarra Tompkins, you are an absolute joy! I had no idea what a Developmental Editor was. Now I'll never write another book without one, and I sure hope you're willing to partner with me on the next one. Grateful for all the hours, days, and finally months you worked on this going above and beyond to make this project the best it could be.

More than anything, I'd like to say thank you to my bride of 28 years. Your influence, your ideas, your insights in the development first as a sermon series, then as a writing project, made it not only so much better, but also more fun than should be called work.

While this book may have my name on the cover, each of you had such a huge part in it. I love teams. Life and work is always so much better when we do them as a family of disciples, chasing Jesus together.

CONTENTS

1

ENOUGH?

What does enough mean to you? Understanding what that word means not only changes how we see God; it also changes how we understand His provision.

As a young man, I had some trouble wrapping my brain around this concept of who our God really is, because I struggled with a performance-based model of faith. I stumbled into this model for my faith, and it took the Holy Spirit to break me free, years later. If you are a military brat or your parents moved you around a lot, then you can understand what it means to be a kid who never really got to build lasting friendships. I am an army brat, the son of an active service member in the United States Army. I was born overseas on an army base in Frankfurt, Germany, and we moved often as we followed my father in his duty assignments. Just as I was about to begin my high school career, we moved to El Paso, Texas. Talk about a change! I walked into a HUGE school on the first day knowing NO ONE. I fell in with the wrong crowd because, honestly, it's the easiest crowd to join.

Based on that influence, I had the opportunity to try my freshman year a second time. Why? Well, I completely failed at my first attempt, thanks to skipping classes and missing assignments. What do you do when your kid can't behave in public school? You send them to private school. My parents had the fantastic idea to send me to a Christian school where it was far more structured. I was surrounded by kids who really wanted to get it right. The peer pressure changed my direction! My teachers and parents helped redirect my focus, and I was able to catch back up and graduate on time. Sounds like a total win, right? Not so fast!

Now let me be clear, I am the son of incredible parents who loved me deeply. That said, they were hugely disappointed by my first freshman year and, with the success I was having at this new school, they thought they had turned me around.

Then one weekend of my senior year, my parents were headed out of town, my brother was already at college, and I had the house to myself. What is a teenage boy supposed to do with an opportunity like this? Throw a party, of course! No worries though, because I was attending a Christian school and most of my friends were from that crowd. It promised to be a pretty tame affair, BUT. I had that one friend (most of us had a friend like this in high school) who said, "I think I can get my hands on a keg of beer."

Not wanting to be "uncool," I said, "Great idea!" Word quickly got out that this party was going to be wild! Here was the prob- lem . . . the word got out. Somebody told a teacher, who told the principal, who placed a phone call to my parents. Mom and Dad left their weekend getaway abruptly and managed to get home right in the middle of the party! Picture every Hollywood teenage party movie with kids bailing out the back door and speeding away as my parents walked in the front door. Their displeasure about cutting their trip short to find a keg party in their house was obvious.

After everyone else had gone, I was left at home with my parents by myself (I really wanted to catch a ride with one of the other kids who were escaping the wrath, but of course I stayed.) It was at that moment that I heard a phrase that almost everyone I've ever met has heard at one point or another. *"I love you, but I don't have to like you right now!"*

Let me reiterate! I had amazing parents! I was deeply and thoroughly loved!

Have you ever heard that phrase? What was the impact it had on you? For me, that phrase, "I love you, but I don't have to like you right now," had me stuck. I KNEW my parents loved me, but I had so disappointed them that IN THAT MOMENT they didn't feel as though they even liked me. If that's how THEY felt, how must GOD feel who knows EVERYTHING? After all, there was more going on than this one party. There were girls, parties in the desert with my OTHER friends who always brought beer (and weed), chores I said that I had done when I hadn't, and on and on and on. I KNEW God loved me, but I was absolutely convinced that there was NO WAY He LIKED me. No way I had His approval. No way He was pleased with me.

How is that connected to having a God that is Enough? Because my picture of God had just been radically changed. Where before I knew that God loved me from every kids' song my mom taught me as a child, ("Jesus Loves Me," "Jesus Loves the Little Children," and on and on), I now saw God as an angry judge or a disappointed teacher because I had been acting up in class. The idea of the God of the universe being displeased with me was crushing! With the weight of all my mistakes pressing down on me, all I could think to do was to find good things, virtuous things, nice things, and *Christian* things to do. I was sure that I could somehow impress God with how hard I was trying to work my way back into His good graces.

Nothing says, "I love God and want to make Him happy" like choosing to attend Oral Roberts University in Tulsa, Oklahoma. Now at this point, I had served the homeless, gone on mission trips, served in kids ministry, served in our church's youth group, and picked a Christian college instead of a party school. To really prove my devotion, once at ORU I joined the men's chaplain program . . . all to try to impress a God who was NOT greater than all I could imagine. He instead was a hyper-accurate accountant keeping a ledger on all my deeds, some good, but mostly not.

Even when I did something good and patted myself on the back, the next thought was an immediate reprimand: "But your motive was wrong, so it didn't count." There was no way out of this war between my human nature and a God who was focused on the smallest detail of my failures. I knew He had mercy and grace . . . but not enough for someone like me.

OUR GOD IS SO MUCH BIGGER AND BETTER THAN THAT!!! Listen to me, if you are feeling this way, you are NOT alone! God wants us to bring these failures to the cross and leave them at the feet of Jesus. In a world that is counting our errors and tabulating our failures, leaving us feeling barren of value, He is more than Enough!

One night during my senior year, all the chaplains were called to an impromptu meeting in a lecture hall. This was irregular, but we were told NOT to miss this meeting. No excuse would be acceptable. We gathered at the appointed time, each of us asking the others if they knew what was up. Our idle chatter turned to silence as a well-known, nationally recognized pastor walked into our meeting. He had dropped by the university, and our campus pastor asked him to speak to our chaplains' program.

He entered the room behind our campus pastor and all the chaplains gasped! Was it really HIM? Once everyone settled into their seats, he began by asking a question. "Who can give me a biblical definition of the word *grace*?"

Remember where I was: at a Christian university. More than that, in a lecture hall of chaplains, most of whom were theology or ministry majors. EVERY HAND (but mine) SHOT UP to answer and impress this great man of God.

The first person he called on gave a VERY impressive definition of grace filled with three and four-syllable words. Surely, THAT answer would impress our speaker and grant the respondent the respect and admiration that he deserved. The guest pastor answered, *"That's good, but that's not what I'm looking for. Who else has an answer?"*

The second person reasonably concluded that the first answer wasn't expository enough, so he outdid the first answer using four and five-syllable words and nearly doubled the length of the answer. The guest pastor answered, *"That's good, but that's not what I'm looking for. Who else has an answer?"*

The THIRD person began an even MORE impressive answer, but after he had been talking for about 30 seconds, the guest pastor interrupted him and said, "I'm not trying to be critical, but I'm looking for a simple answer. Let me just go ahead and give it to you. Grace, simply put, means that right now, right where you are, before you get cleaned up, before you get all your ducks in a row, before you stop this or start that, before you change all your friends, RIGHT NOW, God is crazy about you. He LIKES you right now, in this moment."

This moment changed my life. I was stunned. My entire world stopped spinning. I couldn't even speak. I felt as though all the air had been sucked out of the room and I could barely breathe.

The rest of the evening was a blur. I didn't hear anything else he said. When he fin- **God wanted** ished speaking, my friends wanted to talk about the message, a couple wanted to go **me, mess** get a burger. I tried to politely sprint out of **and all.** the room back to my dorm room where I BAWLED.

"Is that really true?" I prayed. Despite years of studying and burying myself in the Word, I had never realized God wanted me, mess and all. *That would change EVERYTHING about my faith.* A peace that I could never describe settled in my room, and like someone who had been wandering in the desert without water for a lifetime, I just sat there drinking it in.

If that's really true, then God isn't short on love, mercy, or grace. He has more than enough for all of us. Because that IS true, I can serve, love, give, and LIVE from a place of gratitude and honor for a God who doesn't run short on goodness.

So, what does all of this have to do with the word *Enough*? Writing a book wasn't on my bucket list. Instead, I have stepped into something that I believe the Spirit of God showed me that we all need. What you're about to read is the culmination of years upon years (more than I like to admit most of the time) of God patiently renewing my understanding, my foundational understanding, of who our heavenly Father is. He is so much greater than we can ever grasp, and His love for us is greater and more powerful than we can comprehend.

We really do serve a "More Than Enough" kind of God, but we do NOT serve a wasteful God. The truth is that God's mercy, His grace, His joy, His peace (and on and on) will ALWAYS outpace my capacity to contain it.

If we have a more than *Enough* God and He provides *Enough* for our needs, then what do we do with the excess that is left? In Luke 12:16-21, Jesus tells a parable about a wealthy farmer who was blessed with a farm that produced BIG crops. He said, *"What should I do? I don't have room for all my crops."* Talk about first world problems.

He came up with what he thought was a great plan: *"I'll tear down my barns and build bigger ones."*

Let's just say that God wasn't pleased with his solution. Why? Because WE ARE BLESSED TO BE A BLESSING!!! When God pours out His goodness on us, it will be more than we can contain! We are supposed to take the overflow and spread it to those around us as we give God all the glory!

We are blessed to be a blessing!!!

That's not to say that God is against you having nice things; He's against nice things having YOU. He's against a greedy, hoarding spirit in us!

God is so good that He wants to use US to be a blessing to the world!

My life and my perspective of God were changed and from that point forward, I have observed and learned that the God we serve is MORE THAN ENOUGH in so many ways. If you have ever wondered if you are enough or if God is enough, then you are in the very place that God wants you to be. God wants you to fully discover what His Word says about *"Enough."* Let's dive in together and get a new understanding of just who our God is!

PUT IT TO WORK

One of the biggest struggles in the Christian walk can be knowing that God truly accepts you exactly as you are. While it's true that He loves you too much to leave you in that condition, He loves YOU... not some future version of you. He loves YOU... RIGHT NOW.

Have you ever felt like you've gone too far or done too much for God's mercy to handle? Have you felt like God shouldn't accept you? Why?

Romans 5:8 says, "But God showed his great love for us by sending Christ to die for us **while we were still sinners**. That means that while you were still busy committing the sin you are ashamed of... He loved you so much that He chose to pay the price for your freedom. If God really is that deeply in love with you RIGHT NOW, how does that change your approach to living out your faith?

What would it look like to serve God from an overflow of gratitude and joy rather than guilt and shame and trying to somehow earn His approval?

God accepts you just as you are and loves you for all the unique things He made you to be. How does knowing that change the way you see Him?

Enough?

2

ENOUGH TO BEGIN

Then Jesus said, "What is the Kingdom of God like? How can I illustrate it? It is like a tiny mustard seed that a man planted in a garden; it grows and becomes a tree, and the birds make nests in its branches." He also asked, "What else is the Kingdom of God like? It is like the yeast a woman used in making bread. Even though she put only a little yeast in three measures of flour, it permeated every part of the dough." Luke 13:18-21

All beginnings start small, and this moment is no different. Sharing this message has been on my heart for a long time. The world teaches us that small things are insignificant things. In this world of instant everything, we dismiss small things because in order to meet our expectations they must be bigger and better. We don't want small . . . we want BIG!

What makes it worse is the idea that you can't get started on that big dream until you have everything you need. Sometimes it's hard to grasp that what you have in your hands is enough to get started. But WHEN you get started, God will meet you in that place. The little you have will become more than enough.

What He's doing in you is far more important than any miracle you can ask of Him. Maybe you're struggling in a season of job loss, health issues, or some other situation.

Know this: God can answer those needs.

He CAN provide a miracle and when He does, it's great whether He provides a complete miracle in the moment or if He provides in a way that we don't expect. What is WAY more important than a miracle? It is what He is doing inside us. It is Him changing WHO we are, more than just changing our circumstances.

We are going to review a lot of scripture on this journey together (I am sure that is no surprise), but there is something very important that I want you to do when we come to passages from God's Word. Anytime you read a passage of scripture that has so much information to draw from and consider, you can easily get to a point where you're not really connecting with the story anymore. In the overwhelm, you're just reading the words and losing the potential impact they can have. As we read together, I want you to slow down and listen as if you were there.

Our core scripture for this chapter is Luke 13:18-19. I love, love, love reading Luke because instead of it feeling like a technical lesson, it feels like sitting with a friend. This passage from Luke 13 is also reflected in Matthew 13 and in Mark 4; but we're going to start in Luke because I want you to hear it . . . I mean, REALLY hear it!

It is easy to get caught up in the "So-and-so said this and somebody else said that, and they did this other thing." Instead,

Luke is so conversational that you can almost hear Jesus speaking. I love the way Luke writes.

Take just a minute and really picture yourself in the audience in that moment. In this passage Jesus is speaking to His disciples and followers. Imagine you've been raised on the stories of God parting the Red Sea, leading His people out of bondage in Egypt, and then wiping out the entire Egyptian army in one moment as He closed the waters back up. That's just one of SO MANY stories . . . and that wasn't even the Messiah, that was Moses. The Messiah is going to be EVEN GREATER!

Put yourself in His audience because He is also speaking to us. He begins by saying in effect:

"What's the Kingdom of heaven like? What should I compare it to? How can I illustrate it?"

Of course, we'd all be scooting forward and leaning in because after all . . . Jesus, the long-awaited Messiah, the Son of the Living God, is about to tell us what the kingdom of heaven is like, and He would know!

"This is going to be amazing! I can't wait to hear it! He is going to say, 'It's like a giant mountain.' He is going to say, 'It's like a mighty thunder cloud.' He is going to say, 'It's like the roaring oceans.' Tell us, Jesus!"

Instead, Jesus says, "The kingdom of heaven is like a mustard seed."

Wait . . . WHAT?!?

"When a man plants it, it grows into the biggest tree in the garden, and the birds build their nests in its branches."

Okay, Jesus . . . that's not at ALL what I was expecting! Thankfully, Jesus continues,

"What else is the Kingdom of God like?"

"Okay, not really sure what that mustard seed thing was about, but now it's going to get good. Okay, okay, I'm ready. Jesus, hit us."

"It's like a little yeast a woman uses in making bread."

"Okay, seriously? Where's He going with this?"

"It is like a little yeast that a woman put into the dough. And when it's had its full measure of time, it permeates through three measures."

It's a picture of a small thing with a huge impact. And by the way, three measures in today's equivalent would be about six gallons of dough. That is a lot of dough. That little pinch of yeast works through all that dough!

The link between the mustard seed and the leaven is the common and pervasive nature of both. *What do you mean by that?* Well, the tree doesn't spring up the moment it's planted; and leaven doesn't make the whole six gallons of dough rise in a moment! It takes time, it takes faithfulness; and, for us, it takes letting God work in and through us.

If it is too hard for you to imagine these examples, then let me share a personal story of how God works through small beginnings. See, I'd been with another church for almost 20 years—19 years and nine months. In January 2019, as I drove from our church office back home, I began to sense a stirring in my heart. This was one of the times I knew for sure the Holy Spirit was speaking to me because it wasn't at all something I was expecting to hear. *"Lafe, you're not going to make it to 20 years planted where you are."*

Did you ever try to negotiate with the Holy Spirit? My first response was, "No way! I'm going to make 20 years! I'm committed! I'm all in! I'm not a half-measures guy, and I'm going to make 20." But I felt like the Holy Spirit was saying to me, *"Lafe, is the 20-year mark important to you, or to me?"* I was immediately convicted of my own pride.

Even with this new revelation, I didn't know how that was going to shake out. I had no plans to leave my associate pastor position, and I was fully committed to the vision of that church. While my wife, Hope, and I believed God put in our hearts that someday we would pastor our own church, that was not on our horizon in that moment. Things were about to change. Remember the yeast? Hope and I were about to see JUST HOW MUCH the Holy Spirit was on the verge of taking a small thing and permeating our lives with it!

The Holy Spirit didn't clue me in by saying, *"You're not going to make 20 years because I'm about to do a whole new thing for you."* He just left it in the air, and I was really bothered. What do we do when we are bothered, worried, or any other kind of thing? We pray. We laid it at the cross and prayed.

In May (FOUR MONTHS LATER) the lead pastor called us in and said, "We just want to let you know, if it's ever on your heart to start a church, your own church, we want to bless and send you." That shook me. We had prayed that if we were to leave, we wanted to leave in peace and with honor, without any kind of division. We had prayed that God would put it on our pastor's heart to "bless and send us out" (we prayed those exact words). I had never talked about it with him, yet he's the one who brought it up to us... just like we'd asked God. The Holy Spirit was leading us through the whole process. If we were ever going to start a church, we wanted to do it right and with honor, and not just leave to do our own thing. We had prayed that we would be "blessed out" and "sent." He used those exact words! It was nothing shy of amazing!

A few months later we were in San Diego at an Association of Related Churches conference. ARC is an organization that helps plant and launch churches. This conference was where pastors could come and prepare as they begin the process of planting a new church. The more we heard about the success stories other churches were sharing about their own "planting" experience with ARC, the more excited we became.

The conference is really like a two-sided interview, complete with all the paperwork too! We were trying to get to know them. *Do we really want to plant our church with ARC?* All the while they were getting to know us. *Did they want to be a part of what we're doing and what we believe God is doing in us?* (Lots of discussions and interviews, written statements of faith and doctrine, references checked, etc.)

On the last day of the conference, we had THE meeting. This decided if they wanted to move forward with us or part ways.

We got the news we wanted. They were all in and ready to move forward. *Great!* Even better, they seemed really excited about the vision for the church God put on our hearts. There was just one catch. They asked us to consider waiting a year.

I'm sorry . . . What??

When you are at the edge of your seat and ready to launch into God's vision, the word *wait* is devastating. Honestly, that moment broke my heart because I knew the timing was NOW. This was "go" time! If we had to launch without ARC, we'd launch without them. We absolutely knew the timing was now.

The moment we said we were moving forward now, they quickly said that they still wanted to be a part of what we were doing. They warned us though, *"If you launch in only four months, you will probably have a smaller launch. It just isn't enough time to raise funds and build a team. Most people plan for over a year before they launch, and you only have four months."*

We believed God was in this. Without hesitation, we decided to launch in January 2020. In those four months leading up to the birth of Grace Point Family Church, God met every need. We launched debt-free. Everything was paid for! God provided every dollar we would need, and then some. God's provision isn't "Just Enough"; it is more than *Enough!*

God's provision isn't "Just Enough"; it is more than *Enough!*

Romans 8:28 says, "God works all things together for the good." God works all things, especially the small things. Not just the good things either. He will work the painful things and the not-so-great things into something significant. Not only was he taking small things in us, but He was also laying the foundation (not even where we thought He would) to work all things for the significant. We were called to a small town, one that we would never have personally pursued. He spoke into the hearts of the people we met with in providing the exact place of worship. Not a large building, but a school building. He was also preparing the hearts of a small group of people to step into a significant call to His purpose.

We were meeting as a church for seven weeks when the Covid-19 virus hit. One Thursday afternoon, I got a call from the assistant superintendent of the school district where we were meeting. They called to let us know we wouldn't have access to the school until this whole thing was over *("Don't worry, it will probably just be for a couple of weeks")*.

We were advised to shut down and launch again in the fall, but for us, relaunching later was not what I felt God was saying for our small church. It wasn't the direction God had for us. We knew then, it was no longer about us establishing our church. God called us IN THIS SEASON to be His arms and hands extended to our community. We were not going to pull back. We were not going to withdraw. We were not going to catch our breath.

As a church, we were called to do more. During our online service that next Sunday I announced to our church that God had people we could help through a difficult time . . . the response was AMAZING. To say our congregation responded to that call would be a MASSIVE understatement! We were able to minister to hurting families by providing food for people affected by the shutdown. We began doing monthly drive-up food banks, where God performed miracles in multiplying the food to ensure that every family received enough. By God's grace we reached HUNDREDS of families in our community.

God's vision was that we would be the arms and hands of God extended. As a result, our church grew. People tuned in as we streamed our services online from our home. They emailed us to find out how they could be more involved. *What can we do? How can we find out more about your church?*

As donations came in from the community, we poured thousands of dollars into purchasing food. On that Easter Sunday, 14 members of our church went to downtown Dallas and fed the homeless. Our city caught the excitement and people who weren't even a part of our church asked how they could help. Our little church didn't shrink or shut down during the lockdown . . . WE EXPLODED!

We started small, just like a mustard seed. This is just a PART of our story, but there's so much more as we were planted and began growing. Are you ready to take your mustard seed and begin with us?

Let's GO!

PUT IT TO WORK

Understanding that you don't need a detailed plan to start walking with God changes everything. It's incredible to know that you don't have to have it all figured out before you even begin to serve God. He will guide and provide as you go! What YOU need to do... is take a step.

What is one small step you can take towards God right now?

What fears or expectations are holding you back from walking closer with God?

God has a plan and purpose for your life. Instead of trying to figure it all out on your own, what is one thing you can let go of so God can lead you into something new?

ENOUGH

3

ENOUGH TO START SMALL

When you think of heaven, what is the picture that comes to mind? Do you see endless galaxies to explore? Perhaps you see the grand feast Jesus spoke of in Luke, laid out for all to share. When Jesus described heaven, I am sure those listening felt a little more than confused. *Why would they be confused?* They expected the kingdom to be revealed in full power and majesty with the armies of heaven riding out from the clouds, overturning authorities, crushing the evil rulers of the day, and setting up a brand-new kingdom on earth with themselves as the rulers.

Instead, He was very deliberate in His description of the kingdom starting as a small thing because He was demolishing the idea they had about this magnificent AND INSTANT kingdom of God. One illustration wouldn't be enough to pound this false expectation out of their heads. The eternal piece of their expectation was right. The kingdom of God is a kingdom without end, and ultimately, only what's done for THIS kingdom will matter. BUT, first the kingdom had to be worked INTO them (and us), as a revelation of who Jesus is. He wants to walk in a relationship with us. It's going to start small . . . but it won't END small! As a matter of fact, it will never end!

One day the Pharisees asked Jesus, "When will the Kingdom of God come?" Jesus replied, "The Kingdom of God can't be detected by visible signs. You won't be able to say, 'Here it is!' or 'It's over there!' For the Kingdom of God is already among you." Luke 17:20-21

Before we move on, I want to point out two things. First, He's speaking about Himself, that HE is the kingdom of God being revealed to us on earth; but secondly, it's going to have to start inside of us first.

What does that mean? It's ALWAYS going to start small.

Jesus used five illustrations of something small to describe the kingdom of heaven. Does that seem weird to you? After all, it's THE kingdom to end all kingdoms. What do a mustard seed, a little bit of yeast, a hidden treasure, a pearl, and seed sown in a field have in common and why did He take time to paint this picture of something small for His followers? Because it was completely contradictory to what the Jews of the day expected when the Messiah came. They instead expected the Messiah to appear as a king, fully clothed in royalty and power. He would descend from heaven, destroy the enemies of the Jewish people, and restore Israel to its former glory.

When describing the Kingdom of Heaven, Jesus described it as a treasure; but don't think of it as an Indiana Jones treasure. Jesus said the one who found the treasure in the field **quickly** covered it up and went on his way to acquire the field. So, it was a SMALL treasure that didn't take long to cover up. He went on to describe the kingdom of heaven as a pearl (but don't imagine a pearl the size of a Buick; it's a normal-sized pearl . . . but it has GREAT value). Another description Jesus used for the Kingdom of Heaven was the seed sown in a farmer's field. After the seed is planted and cared for, it reaps a huge harvest—ten, thirty, even a hundredfold.

> **It is time for us, as the body of Christ, to be a part of the solution.**

This means that right now the kingdom of heaven is at work inside of us. Right now! We need to be operating like we believe what we say we believe. If we don't, we can never experience growth into someone who meets the needs of others. It is just one of the many reasons that I'm so excited for YOU to continue reading this book. It is time for us, as the body of Christ, to be a part of the solution. We have a call on our lives to take the small offerings within us and allow God to grow them into a harvest to meet the needs of others, like feeding the homeless or the school lunch program.

In this church-building journey, we have been blessed to open a food pantry where people can come in to select the foods they need. We're aligning with others as we move to be the vessel that God can use for such a time as this. We want to be people available for God to use because the kingdom of heaven is being worked into us. THEN it works its way THROUGH us. THEN God's glory and God's power are on display. No matter how ready we are to do big things for God's kingdom, we must remember that it must start in us in seed form.

There's a problem with small . . . It's hard to grasp.

You may be reading this thinking, "I don't need a small thing right now. I need Jesus to show up in a big, powerful way right now!" Let me tell you: He can answer prayers and show up in the middle of your mess; but ultimately, He wants to do something incredible IN you that He will eventually work THROUGH you!

If you think it is hard to grasp this idea of small things, imagine Jesus is sitting with His followers and you are there. His disciples have the closest seats to Him while He tells a story about the kingdom of heaven as being like something very small. What does He mean by that? They didn't get it.

"Come on, how do you know they didn't get it?" I am so glad you asked!

Soon after this conversation with His followers, Jesus slipped quietly away with the disciples toward the town of Bethesda. But the crowds found out where He was going, and they followed Him. Jesus welcomed them and taught them about the kingdom of God and healed those who were sick. Late in the afternoon, the twelve disciples asked Him to send the crowds away to the nearby villages and farms so the people could find food and lodging for the night. There was nothing to eat in this remote place.

But Jesus said, *"You feed them."*

What I wouldn't give to have seen their faces. Imagine their confusion.

"But we have only five loaves of bread and two fish," they answered. "Or are you expecting us to go and buy enough food for this whole crowd?" Luke 9:13

There were about 5,000 men plus women and children. Jesus instructed the disciples to have them sit down in groups of about 50 each. Notice the large group was divided into small groups. He took the five loaves and the two fish, looked up toward heaven, and blessed the loaves and fish.

Now watch this!!!

If we had been Jesus, we might have done it differently. We'd bless the loaves and fishes and then miraculously, in a display of all the power of heaven, the five loaves would become 5,000 loaves. The two fish would become a mountain of fish. EVERYONE WOULD BE AMAZED! But that's not how He did it.

Instead, He took what was little (not nearly enough) and then He broke that INTO EVEN SMALLER pieces.

He kept giving the bread and the fish to the disciples so they could be distributed. He kept passing it out, and it never seemed to end. There was always more. He kept passing it out, and passing it out, and passing it out! The disciples would take the food from His hands and go give it away and every time they came back, He had more to give them. Everyone ate as much as they wanted. Afterward, the disciples picked up 12 baskets of leftovers. There was more than enough! All they had to do was to keep coming back to Jesus!

A couple of things to consider about this story:

When Jesus said, "You feed them," He wasn't teasing them or taunting them. They really could have, if they had caught the message about beginning small. They could have said, "Absolutely. We don't have much, but let's start with what we have and see what God does."

They didn't do that because their eyes were on the size of their resource, not on the size of their Savior who was walking with them. What good were five loaves and two fish among a crowd of this size? Why even bother starting?

They were willing to do nothing with the little they had, because they believed what they had was not enough. How often do we find ourselves unwilling to start because we haven't amassed everything we believe we need to be successful? Please understand the weight of this. Maybe you're like the disciples and you're looking at your need. What you have isn't much. And as a matter of fact, if it's like the yeast, it's kind of gross.

"God, you're going to use yeast? What we have is not enough to even get started. So why bother?"

But with God, HIS little is more than enough in your situation. He tells us that if we're faithful with the small things we have, He will make us ruler over much (see Matthew 25:23).

But what if I don't even know WHAT to do?

Consider the story of the prophet Ezekiel found in Ezekiel 37:1-14. Ezekiel is taken by the Spirit of God and shown a vision of a valley of dry bones. God asks Ezekiel, "Can these bones live again?" It was at this moment that this champion of faith, this prophet of God, gives one of the WORST answers in the Bible.

"Only you know, God."

If he had said, "*Just say the word and they'll do a lot more than just live!*" . . . that would have been faith. If he had at least said, *"Probably not, they look pretty dead to me . . . "* that would have been a place to start from. Sadly, what he said required no faith, and didn't commit him one way or the other. Thankfully, God was patient and told Ezekiel where to stand and what to say to see a miracle!

How great, how wonderful, and how merciful is our God that when we don't know what to say or do, He gives us not only His power and authority to do the kind of miracles that can only come from Him, but He does it through us. He even gives us the words to say, and tells us where to stand and what we're going to see when we do it.

Maybe right now you're feeling small, and you're over-whelmed because you're looking at the size of the need and not the size of your God. He multiplies your resources until it's not only *just* enough, but *more* than enough.

Let me take you someplace completely different for just a moment. Maybe you're on the other side of the fence, thinking, "I've got way too big a vision. I can't bother with the small things because they don't merit my time."

I remember a time when our former church was planning a mission trip to Skid Row in Los Angeles. A young woman, interested in going, inquired what the team would be doing on the trip. We described the ministry work of feeding the homeless, conducting a VBS-style ministry for the kids, giving the people encouragement from heaven to take the next step forward, and telling them God loves them and sees them in the middle of their pain.

God starts small and helps us grow from the inside into the large vision He has for us.

Much to our surprise, she informed us that she wouldn't be going because the mission didn't seem very impressive. She believed she had a calling to speak to large audiences of thousands and even thousands of thousands, and couldn't see how this boots-on-the-ground experience would be worthy of that.

God starts small and helps us grow from the inside into the large vision He has for us.

When you're faithful in the small things, God meets you in that place. He doesn't want to deal with only the masses of tens of thousands. He wants to reach the one and if you will not go for the one, you will never get the chance to reach the tens of thousands or even hundreds of thousands, because you need to be faithful where He sends you first.

If you think about it, the Bible is replete with stories of small beginnings.

- Five loaves and two fish are way too small a resource to feed 5,000 men plus women and children. But when they're put in God's hands, it's more than enough. Twelve baskets were left over after feeding 5,000. Another time, seven baskets were left over after feeding 4,000. More than enough.

- Five smooth stones against a nine-foot-tall giant with a spear, a sword, and a shield. The small shepherd boy running at him with five smooth stones is way too small to affect the outcome. But again, it's more than enough, because God only needs one of the five stones. The first one is all He needs. A little put in God's hands is more than enough.

- A baby born in a manger in an out-of-the-way rural town is way too small to change the world, but that's exactly what He did.

Think about Zechariah 4:10.

Don't despise these small beginnings for the Lord rejoices to see the work begin, to see the plumb line in Zerubbabel's hand.

The people of that time rebuilt the wall around Jerusalem, but their joy and celebration turned to sorrow when they realized they couldn't fulfill the law of Moses. How often do we let something that seems unfinished steal the joy of the small beginnings we bravely started when God called us?

In our own strength, it's too much. But the joy of the Lord is our strength in this day of small beginnings. In other words, God began with them where they were, and then empowered them to take the next step.

What's in your hand today? What would represent a step toward God for you today? If it seems like it's not enough, you can put it in God's hands. Ask God if that will be enough. The amazing thing is He will say yes. He'll meet you in that place.

Maybe you want to follow God. You felt God calling you, but you know you're not much of a reader, and the Bible seems like too much. You don't even know where to begin. Think about this! A small start for you would be the 31 chapters of Proverbs. There are 31 days in a month. Start with whatever day it is. For example, on the 19th read Proverbs 19. That's your proverb for the day. If you miss a day, you don't have to catch up. Just pick up with the chapter that corresponds to the next date. You'll catch up with the missed proverb next month. In one month, you're reading the book of wisdom from front to back. It's a great place to start when building your faith.

Maybe you're saying, "I know I need to pray, but I heard that Jesus asked the disciples, *'Could you not tarry with me one hour?'* An hour seems like a lot because, honestly, I run out of things to say in about five minutes." Pray for five minutes! Take what you have in your hand and put it in God's hands. Pray the five minutes, and tomorrow shoot for six. We don't have to imagine that in one moment in time, we need to start living a sinless, perfect life. The truth is, we'll never get there. We will never be good enough to earn it on our own. We won't measure up. The good news is His grace interrupts us and says, *"You can't do it on your own, but I can. I'm going to give you my righteousness as if you've earned it for yourself."*

What do you have today? "Well, I'm supposed to love my neighbor, but I really can't stand him." Or, "There's a guy at work that bugs me." A small step for you today is to say something kind to him, to be gracious and merciful. Even when he may have been a jerk to you.

What's a small thing that's in your hands? You have resources. It doesn't seem like enough but put it in God's hands. He will make it more than enough. What can you put in God's hands as you're reading this? If you start there, He'll meet you there. And trust me, it will be more than enough.

PUT IT TO WORK

God is always faithful, and you can trust in His goodness. In return, when you are faithful with the small things, He will show you what incredible things can happen.

Ephesians 3:19 and 20 says, "May you experience the love of Christ, though it is too great to understand fully. Then you will be made complete with all the fullness of life and power that comes from God. **Now all glory to God, who is able, through his mighty power at work within us, to accomplish infinitely more than we might ask or think.**

Have you ever considered that God might have more in mind for your story than you've even imagined? Remember though, it's all for HIS glory, not our ego.

What is one small step that you could take today? This could be as simple as reading your Bible every day, or sharing the things God is doing in your life with others.

How will this step impact you or others?

Your impact on the kingdom is much bigger than you can believe. It will always start small, but it won't STAY small… and it will always be remarkable!

4

ENOUGH FAITHFULNESS

When we understand clearly why God starts small, we'll understand the power, majesty, and beauty of His kingdom. We can't take it lightly. It cannot be an instant thing. This is not a "pop it in the microwave" item that is done in two minutes. This is something that must be worked into the heart of who we are. It is the kingdom of God.

This isn't easy Christianity. It requires letting go of the thinking, "I'm safe now. Nothing bad is ever going to happen. I'll just welcome blessings wherever I go. No problem is ever going to come my way because, after all, I'm a Christian now."

Instead, it begins WITHIN us. We need to accept that He's going to refine us, helping us to grow, develop, and strengthen our faith. It is going to be a process that we must walk through. That process almost always involves some challenge or obstacle that we must overcome. That's the nature of a process. It requires something from us.

God is, right now, within us and for us. Maybe you don't feel like that. Maybe you're going through some hard things and don't understand how God could possibly be present. Let me assure you, He is with you, and He is for you RIGHT NOW.

God is, right now, within us and for us.

Even if you don't understand how, the kingdom of God is within you. As we walk it out and grow in this process of God maturing us as believers, we will begin to experience that the kingdom of God really is in us. What's even better is how He is going to express it through us. Some of that understanding begins with His faithfulness.

What is faithfulness? The 1828 American Dictionary of the English Language describes it as: *a firm allegiance and duty. Strict performance of promises, vows, or covenants.* While a definition is easy to read, it's usually something we see in hindsight. It's making and keeping our commitments. It's choosing to work through our challenges and not giving up.

Speaking of challenges...

Let me share a story about my sweet bride:

How many times have you moved in the last five years? Well, imagine the idea of moving your wife five times in the first year of marriage. It's amazing that she even chose to stay with me!

Plans always change, and when we first got engaged, we planned to move to Dallas because my company was going to transfer me there. After college, we moved her to Dallas where she lived with her family. When the wedding day arrived, the transfer still hadn't come. So, after the honeymoon, we loaded up my truck. (It looked like the Clampetts moving to Beverly Hills. If you are too young for the reference, just Google it!) We had everything tied down and strapped down and we were praying the whole time that nothing would fall off. We gathered up all her belongings and we headed back to Tulsa where we rented a house and unpacked. While I worked, my sweet wife poured her heart into unpacking and decorating, and she made that rental house beautiful!

What came next sounds like fiction, but it is literally what happened, no exaggeration needed!

Just weeks after the move I came home from work and said, "Hey, honey! Great news."

"I've got great news too!" she exclaimed.

"What's your great news?" I asked.

"I finished unpacking the very last box and on top of that, I got rid of all the boxes! The last picture is hung on the wall, and we're done!" She was glowing with accomplishment. Then I had to burst her bubble.

"Wow! That's awesome! (Pause for dramatic effect.) The transfer came through."

We again prayed about it and accepted the transfer. We repacked everything she had just completed unpacking. We rented a box truck and moved it all back to Dallas.

One problem, the rental home we found in North Dallas wasn't ready yet.

So, for six weeks we lived with my in-laws in their guest room. It was a wonderful blessing because my in-laws are amazing. At the end of the six weeks our rent house was finally ready, so we moved . . . again.

By the end of the first year back in Dallas, we had found a home we wanted to buy. Our very first purchase of a home managed to fall within that same year. So, we moved ONE MORE TIME. This time into our new home. The amazing thing about these five moves is that with every one of them, Hope made it our home. She unpacked, she decorated. She could have fussed and done what I would have done.

If it were me, I'd look at all the work that I knew was temporary and say, "I'm good." And leave everything in boxes. "Just let me know when we're done moving." Until then I'd leave it where it was.

Not Hope. My sweet bride is so wonderful that she made every place feel like our home. She decorated, she made it beautiful, she made it home.

She's amazing, and that to me is such a testament of faithfulness.

During that time, I had one job. Besides unpacking and decorating, she had three different jobs. She had a teaching position lined up in Dallas. It's a big deal when the teacher asks to leave in the middle of a contract. But when we moved her back to Tulsa, she got a teaching position there. Then she had to walk away from the Tulsa contract and start interviewing again in Dallas. She interviewed for and worked three different jobs in one year.

From small beginnings we move into the power of faithfulness.

Again. To recap, she had to move us FIVE times and get THREE jobs in the space of one year. That is amazing! That speaks to me so loudly of faithfulness. From small beginnings we move into the power of faithfulness.

Once you and I yield our lives to Christ we move from small beginnings into the danger zone. It's the danger zone because this is where so many quit. Why? Perhaps they have expectations of easy living. Many get discouraged along the way, and still for others they lose their focus on our Savior.

It's important to stay focused on God because now we're in the middle and this is where things start happening. *What kind of things?* I am so glad you asked.

Anytime we listen to a story, watch a movie, or read a book, it's the middle where things get rough; and the story begins to shift. In the first couple of chapters, you hopefully meet some great characters with compelling backstories and begin to care about what happens to them. When the middle of the book comes . . . things go wrong.

- The villains come into the picture.

- There are obstacles to overcome.

- There are unexpected attacks.

- There is loss and heartache.

- There are lessons learned.

These events cause the characters to grow and of course lead us to the best part—the end! Reaching the end is always fun because the conflict we have been swimming in has reached its conclusion. You can now see the story with perfect clarity and understand where the author was going the entire time. Before you can get to that resolution you have to go through the middle, and the middle is messy.

The middle requires faithfulness! It's going to require something of us, but if you'll embrace the process, the middle is where things get really exciting! *Okay, are you trying to convince me that in the middle, where the mess is, where things are the hardest, that is where I can expect amazing things?*

To that I answer you with a resounding YES! As you begin to walk in faith, you give God the space to do incredible things! In the beginning, faithfulness through the mess may seem like a chore, a duty, or even an obligation. How many times have you been in a Bible study just going through the motions? As with any habit, good or bad, it is easy for us to put our faith on auto-pilot. As we get into God's Word and begin exercising our faith, something miraculous happens. We begin to understand that it's the PROCESS that's beautiful. We move in faith and take a step, then God meets us in that place and directs our NEXT step. We step again, and He is faithful to meet us there too. Step by step, He takes us to the next level.

Faithfulness is required to grow those small beginnings. Remember our core scriptures from Luke. Jesus gave five different illustrations of starting small:

- the mustard seed

- a little leaven

- a treasure in a field

- a pearl

- a farmer's seed for his crops

Have you ever made bread before? Even a small loaf requires many steps. Including waiting. If we look back at the leaven, Jesus said the woman buried it in the dough and then she left it. It was not instant. It had to have its full measure of time before all six gallons of dough had risen.

This process takes time. We live in a world where everything is at our fingertips all the time. It creates within us the need to have instant results. Instant drive through, instant microwave, instant everything. Understand that what has been put in us will be accomplished if we do our part. God will begin to work in us, and over time our results are going to be revealed.

We will reap a harvest. So, what does that mean? For example, if you bury a mustard seed in the ground and walk away and forget it, probably nothing will happen. You must break up the right kind of ground and make sure it gets plenty of water. We must make sure that it has the right conditions. That's our part. If we do that, a mustard tree grows and becomes the largest tree in the garden. (It can grow to 20 feet across and 20 feet tall.)

If you put the leaven into six gallons of dough and then stick it in the fridge, probably not a lot is going to happen. We must be careful of our expectations. As we're walking this out, it's going to require something of us. The link is the pervasive nature of both. When our process has its full measure of time and the right conditions, and when we've done our part, there's an amazing harvest.

So how long is the full measure of time?

That's a great question with a not-so-great answer! I have no idea! What I do know is if we aren't faithfully doing our part, it will take much, much longer.

Okay, but how will I recognize it when my process begins?

I promise you . . . it already has! It may not look like much now, but when you are faithful with what is in your hands today, you are qualifying yourself for your tomorrow. One of the greatest difficulties with this process is that we are waiting for the right time or the right circumstance to begin. "I'll make my growth/my goal a part of my new year's resolutions next year," or "I'll start putting real effort in when I get a better job."

Have you ever felt like that? Or maybe you know God has great plans and purpose for you, but you are waiting for HIM to begin, or to provide you with all the resources you will need before you begin.

In other words, we are waiting for real life to begin. The story goes like this:

I was always looking forward to the time when my real life would begin. At first, I thought it would be when I graduated from high school. Then I thought it would be when I went off to college. During my studies in college I thought, "No, it's when I graduate from college." After graduation it had to be when I get my first real job.

This list could go on forever. Your "real life" starts right now! Right this very minute! What is stopping you from embracing your real life? One of our biggest hurdles to accepting is that we fail to enjoy the journey, the adventure God has for us in the process. Maybe it doesn't feel much like an adventure. Maybe it feels like a routine. Maybe you feel like you are trapped in a daytime TV drama. Ask God to give you a new perspective. Ask the Holy Spirit to help you see the opportunities to make a difference in the lives of those around you everywhere you go. Just because you are in a process doesn't mean that happiness is something to be reserved for when you've reached your destination because here's the thing, we never get to our destination! As long as you're still drawing breath, you still have a purpose and God still has a plan. There's more in front of you! If you wait till later to enjoy the journey, you never will!

As long as you're still drawing breath, you still have a purpose and God still has a plan.

FINDING JOY IN THE NOW

My son was in his junior year in college when the Covid shutdown began. He came home for spring break and never got to go back to campus. As if in an instant, everything switched to online learning. The teachers assigned the students more and more work to ensure what they would have taught in the classroom was really being understood. That meant the workload for all the students had gone way, way, way up.

My son was pushing through the late hours of the night. There were times we got up in the morning and he was still awake. He went to bed at 6:30-7:00 in the morning because he worked all night long on a project or a paper. In that season, my son was perpetually frustrated and tired due to what felt like endless deadlines. If you listened to him talk, you could hear it, *"This week I'm really pushing hard because I've got a midterm."* Then, *"I've got another project to do especially now that all the classes are online."* His answer was always, *"I can rest and enjoy life once I get past this deadline."* Yet, without fail, the next week brought something else, and he'd have to push a little harder.

We do the same thing. If you think about it, you might re-member saying something like, "If I just push through this little season right now, then on the other side I can relax. Then life will get better. Then I can take it easy. Then I'm going to be blessed and favored." We struggle to understand that if we're not careful, we'll always move happiness a little farther over the horizon. And, yes, we must let the leaven do its work. We need to understand that it's all a part of God doing something in us, which means we need to give it time. However, the blessing, the favor, and the kingdom of God are on you right now!

Even when we go through challenges and are faced with ob-stacles in our way, God is faithful. If we'll be faithful too, there's absolutely going to be a harvest. So, the kingdom of heaven starts small, but it must grow and be cultivated by application and revelation. When we mature and are faithful with what's put in our hands, everything, everything, everything changes.

So let's not get tired of doing what is good. At just the right time we will reap a harvest of blessing if we don't give up (Galatians 6:9).

The difficult thing about that verse is that it's so easy to get tired of doing the right things when we're in the middle of the process . . . when we've been holding on and doing our best, but the harvest seems to be delayed.

When we get weary or frustrated, our response should be, "God, right now, in this moment, you're with me in this journey and doing something in me that's beautiful. If I give it the measure of time, if I'll be faithful to do my part, I might see heaven revealed like I could never imagine any other way."

In Matthew 25 Jesus gives us another picture. He's going to take us a little deeper.

He tells us the kingdom can be illustrated by the story of a man going on a long trip. He calls together his servants and entrusts his money to them while he is gone. He gave five bags of silver to one, two bags of silver to another, and a bag of silver to the last, based on what he knew of their abilities. And he then left on his trip.

The servant who received five bags of silver began to invest the money and earned five more. The servant with two bags of silver earned two more. But the servant who received one bag of silver dug a hole in the ground and hid his master's money.

After a long time, the master returned from his trip and called them to give an account of how they'd used his money. The servant to whom he entrusted five bags of silver came forward with five more bags and said, "Master, you gave me five bags of silver to invest. I've earned five more." The master was full of praise.

"Well done, my good and faithful servant. You have been faithful in handling this small amount, so now I will give you many more responsibilities. Let's celebrate together!"
Matthew 25:23

Wait a second. Are you telling me their reward for doing a good job was more responsibilities? Yes, but when you embrace what God is doing, it's a joy. You were made for this when you're walking in what God has called you to be and do. There's no deeper level of joy.

By the way, my call is not the same as your call. Don't compare, and don't be intimidated by the idea of more responsibilities.

Whatever God has for you will be the most joyful thing you can imagine. It might not be easy, but you will come alive whenever you're faithfully working to accomplish the purpose that God created for you. It will fulfill you and excite you like nothing else could. So, the reward for faithfulness is greater capacity.

That's true of everything. When you get a promotion at work, you don't get less responsibility given to you; you get more. If you work out at a gym, you consistently increase the weights or time of exercise.

You are made for this. God is going to give you more joy, and yes, more capacity than you can imagine. The servant who received two bags of silver also earned two more. The master also rewarded him with more responsibilities and celebration. Then the servant with one bag of silver told the master that he knew him to be a harsh man who harvests crops he didn't plant and gathered crops he didn't cultivate. He was afraid of losing what little he had, so he buried it, then gave it back to his master.

But the master called him wicked and lazy!

"Why didn't you deposit my money in the bank? At least I could have gotten some interest on it" (Matthew 25:27).

He took the money from this servant and gave it to the one with ten bags of silver.

"To those who use well what they're given, they will have abundance. But from those who do nothing, even what little they have will be taken away." Matthew 25:29

If you've been around church or been a believer for any time at all you've heard this story in scripture. This is not new to you. If you're like me at all, this passage caused you some anxiety as you questioned within yourself whether you were a five-talent servant, a two-talent servant, or heaven forbid, a one-talent servant.

The important thing to remember is that the outcome for the five and two-talent servants was the same: They doubled what they were given because they put it to good use. I know that for a while, I questioned whether I might even be a one-talent servant because I wondered if I was putting to good enough use what I'd been given. Worse yet, perhaps I didn't even understand what my talent was, and therefore, wasn't even using it. Here's what I've learned and want you to understand. You are a five-talent servant because God has given each of us more than enough talents to work with.

- If you can lift your voice in praise, that's a talent. I'm not talking about being a great singer, but rather the ability to worship at all.

- If God's given you friends, family, or loved ones in your life, that's a talent. If you treat them with love and honor and encourage them in the Word, that's a talent.

- If you have the ability to work, that's a talent.

- If you have the ability to reach the lost or serve people in need, that's a talent.

- If you can encourage those around you, that's a talent.

The truth is that we could list a whole lot more, but that's five talents right here. So be clear: You are a five-talent servant. Whatever you do, do it with the attitude of working for the Lord. He is faithful to multiply your effort.

Work willingly at whatever you do, as though you were working for the Lord rather than for people. Colossians 3:23

He doesn't force your hand on any of it. He doesn't make you praise Him. You choose to do that. You can praise Him and put that talent to work, or you can bury it. He doesn't force you to love your family. He's not going to force you to go to work. He's not going to force you to get jobs, better jobs, raises, or bonuses. He's not going to force you to do that. But you have talents and opportunities. That's exactly what the master did when he went on a long journey, and he left his servants with talents. He gave them an opportunity to excel. You're a five-talent person. Don't see yourself as anything less.

The parable of talents, then, is about faithfulness. What distinguished the five and two-talent servants? It was their faithfulness in putting to use what was entrusted to them. And they both doubled what they were given. The one-talent servant wasn't punished because he lost the talent. He gave it back in full. The judgment came because he hadn't been faithful in using what he'd been given. Why don't we strive to live and give to the fullest of our abilities? What would hold us back?

Fear is the chief enemy of faithfulness.

The answer is usually fear. Fear is the chief enemy of faithfulness. It is the great immobilizer. It has frozen many people in their tracks and kept them from accomplishing all that they were created to do. During World War II, fear caused the government of India to hoard rice in a fortified city so the Japanese couldn't come and take it. They never came. Millions outside that city died of starvation throughout India in 1943. There wasn't a lack of food, but fear kept it away from the people who needed it most.

- Fear caused the Israelites to grumble and complain as God was delivering them from the pharaoh's armies.

- Fear froze the armies of Israel as they faced Goliath.

- Fear caused disciples to wake Jesus in the middle of a storm on the sea.

- Fear caused Peter to deny Jesus before His crucifixion.

Fear immobilizes people who focus on their lack and not God's faithfulness to sustain us.

What does faithfulness look like? Consider the early church.

It started small, in an upper room with 120 men and women. When the Holy Spirit fell on them, they immediately went out from that place, shared the news about Jesus, and thousands were added. That's a great start! But soon persecution began. They went into hiding, meeting in homes. The Roman officials imprisoned believers, tortured them, and found ridiculous ways to kill them. They put them in arenas with lions and tigers to dissuade others from joining this new movement.

From the outside, this new church looked frail, one blow away from being wiped off the face of the earth. But God uses small things to change everything. Instead of crushing the early church, the persecution caused it to explode! The people were faithful and didn't give up in the face of persecution, hardship, or hunger. These witnesses saw the light and stepped out in faith, overcoming obstacles along the way.

What can we do to model what the early church taught us?

- Be ready to tell others about the hope that you've found.

- Serve. Serve in every way you can. Serve the lost, the hungry, and the hurting.

Maybe you're thinking, "But I'm hurting! I'm the one who needs encouragement."

Let me tell you the very best thing you can do in this moment is to find someone to serve and encourage. Maybe they aren't even as bad off as you are. Serve them anyway! God gets in the middle of our messes when we love and serve as his arms and hands extended.

God is always faithful. If you activate the talent of generosity, you'll excite the heart of God. He'll find a way to bless you. You can't pour water from a vase without getting the vase wet. Generosity isn't only about money. It's being part of advancing the kingdom of God on earth. Find somebody to serve and encourage. God gets involved when we start small. It takes root and grows.

Start small, be faithful, and grow big!

PUT IT TO WORK

Being a Christian doesn't mean we've been promised a safe or easy life. In fact, in John 16:33, we are promised the opposite from Jesus Himself. Being a Christian also doesn't mean everyone will like you. At some point, people will be unkind because of your faith.

What are some of the difficult times in life that have made you question your faith?

God can use those times and take the hardest and most painful moments of your story and make them a powerful part of who you are called to be.

How will your faith be changed by understanding Romans 8:28? Understanding that God uses even the hard times in our story can make it easier to have gratitude when those tough times do come.

Will that make it easier to walk in gratitude when tough times do come?

5

ENOUGH MERCY

As a Pastor it's really important to spend a little extra time in preparing your Mother's day message. Yes, we want to celebrate the mothers in our church, but it's much more complicated than easy celebration of motherhood. Some are struggling because they've lost their mothers. For others, they struggle because the relationship they have with the mothers in their life might not be great. For many though, it's hard for a whole different reason. There's just not much simple about being a mom or dad. If you're like me at all, there are times when I look back and cringe. Times when I was too hard on my kids, or I was too easy on them when I should have been more disciplined in correcting behavior. There are times I will look back and think, "I wish I had handled that better. I wish

> **Grace is unmerited favor, and undeserved privilege.**

I had been gentler and had a softer answer." Or, "I should have held them more accountable."

As a dad, there are times that I really struggle. It's hard. I celebrate all the wins along the way, but I also struggle with remembering ways I should've done better. Our shortcomings are not news to God. We mess up. God knows it. Grace is unmerited favor, and undeserved privilege. Jesus paid the price, and we get the reward. So, if you ever struggle with insecurity or ways that you've fallen short or blown it like I have, take heart! You and I are like the apostle Paul.

The examples and illustrations we're going to use for this chapter on Mercy are centered around parenthood, but when we come to God in earnest repentance, the mercy of God makes up for what we lack in ANY area of our lives. Paul was never a parent, but he knew what it meant to fall on the mercy of God.

Paul was very much aware of his own faults and shortcomings, and he asked God to take his faults away three times; but in 2 Corinthians 12:9, the response from God was, "My grace is sufficient." You won't ever be perfect; you will mess up, but when you mess up, the good news from heaven is His grace is sufficient!

Paul said he had been given a thorn in the flesh to keep him humble. You may be struggling with something too. Each and every one of us will fall. It isn't if, but when. The key to finding His strength in this is accepting His grace.

When we are too weak to do what needs to be done, then God's power is made perfect in your life and mine. We move from self-reliance to God-reliance. We are forced to rely on Him. This is why His grace is so important. I love that God's response when you mess up (and you will) is to get back up!

Don't think for a second that God doesn't know you inside and out. My God knows me so well. He knows where I'm weak. He's not surprised by it. He's not taken off guard by it. God is not frustrated by me. When I'm too weak to accomplish what God has for me to accomplish, I must rely solely on God. That's what makes grace so vital to my faith.

This is a big, big, big deal. Why? Read this twice. His grace is what I fall on when I'm not enough. I'm imperfect. I'll never be enough on my own. I'm always going to have to rely on the grace and the goodness of God.

There was a time when my wife and I were out of the house, and Callie (our oldest daughter) decided to make some tapioca pudding. We had a glass stovetop and somehow or another, the tapioca spilled out of the pan and onto the glass stovetop and it cracked. Okay, so cracked isn't exactly the right word . . . it split and caved in! Let's just say it was no longer usable. Completely destroyed. Can't cook on it. Callie was beyond upset.

She kept apologizing and expected us to be upset and angry. When we mess up, many times we think God is going to be angry with us. Instead of seeing God as loving, merciful, and grace giving, we reduce Him to a teacher who gives out bad grades on a report card. God knows our pain inside and out. Callie expected wrath when we came home and saw the stove, but I know my daughter. I know she didn't mean to break the stove.

You cannot exhaust the goodness, the mercy, and the grace of our God.

We hugged her and said, "Baby, it's okay. We'll take care of it."

Just like we understood Callie's pain, God knows ours.

I've asked God to forgive me multiple times. At the time, I felt sure I'd worn out His patience. I thought He must be done with me. But what He will tell me, and you, from the heart of heaven is His grace is sufficient. If there is an area of weakness where you just don't feel like you're enough, there's great news.

God's grace is more than enough if you've blown it. Even if you've blown it for the hundredth time. Or if you think you've blown it beyond repair. You cannot exhaust the goodness, the mercy, and the grace of our God. Grace, and mercy, and love, and compassion, and peace, and faithfulness, and goodness! There's always more than enough.

Are you familiar with the British writer and theologian C.S. Lewis? He was one of the intellectual giants of the twentieth century, and one of the most influential writers of his day. He was the author of *The Chronicles of Narnia* and *Mere Christianity,* among several others. I love, love, love his books. I love his writings and his essays.

We serve an infinite God, and there's always more than enough.

When asked, "What makes Christianity different from all the other religions of the world?" he immediately commented, "Oh, that's easy. It's grace." Grace is unmerited favor. Grace is also when we choose not to judge or condemn someone else. We give them grace. It's that second definition that makes grace and mercy seem like synonyms, but they are not.

Mercy is when we **don't get** what we **do** deserve.

Grace is when we **do get** what we **don't** deserve.

You can't beat the definition that Max Lucado shares. "Mercy gave the Prodigal Son a second chance. Grace gave him a feast."

Mercy is not getting a punishment that we deserve. Grace is getting a reward when it was truly Jesus who earned it, not us. The truth is that we can't earn grace; it's way too big for us to earn. Jesus paid a price we cannot pay. And then we're the ones who receive what He paid for in full.

The power of God is made available to you! If you are struggling with the issues of life, God's power is available because His grace is sufficient. We serve an infinite God, and there's always more than enough.

Therefore, since we have been made right in God's sight by faith, we have peace with God because of what Jesus Christ our Lord has done for us. Because of our faith, Christ has brought us into this place of undeserved privilege where we now stand, and we confidently and joyfully look forward to sharing God's glory. Romans 5:1-2

Read verse 2 again where it says Christ brought us to undeserved privilege. Really let it sink in. That is the very definition of grace. Paul doesn't say "undeserved privilege" timidly, with guilt and shame, for us to observe but not be allowed to participate in God's glory.

Have you struggled and maybe thought you've just done too much wrong—you've gone too far? It's not too far for God's grace.

The apostle Paul said that because of grace we confidently and joyfully look forward to sharing in God's glory! *Confidently* and *joyfully* stand out to me. We are brought into a place of honor as a child of God, and now we confidently and joyfully look forward to sharing with God.

God's law was given so that all people could see how sinful they were. But as people sinned more and more, God's wonderful grace became more abundant. So just as sin

---

ruled over all people and brought them to death, now God's wonderful grace rules instead, giving us right standing with God, and resulting in eternal life through Jesus Christ our Lord. Romans 5:20-21

So just as sin ruled over all people and brought them to death, now God's wonderful grace rules instead. This gives us right standing with God and results in eternal life through Jesus Christ.

Mercy is beautiful and it's amazing. It's forgiveness of sin. When you've earned a penalty or consequence, when you've fallen short and you know you deserve punishment, mercy says God forgives sin. But grace takes it one step further.

God's grace is sufficient in supply. Sufficient means you can never exhaust it.

- How many gallons of seawater are in the ocean? The answer is 3.612 times 10 to the 20th power gallons. That's 3.612 with 21 zeros following. That number is provided by oceanographers, ocean ecologists, ocean scientists, ocean people who study the ocean.

- How many stars are in the known universe? The answer is 70 sextillion (7 followed by 22 zeros) calculated by a team of astronomers at the Australian National University.

- How many grains of sand are in the world? It is 7,500,000,000,000,000,000, or seven quintillion 500 quadrillion grains of sand.

These numbers are so huge it's hard for our minds to grasp. God's grace is even bigger than these numbers and then the grace of God is just getting started.

I love this quote from Charles Spurgeon.

When God forgives our sins, there's more forgiveness to follow. He justifies us in the righteousness of Christ, but there's more to follow. He adopts us into his family, but there's more to follow. He prepares us for heaven, but there's more to follow. He gives us grace, but there's more to follow. He helps us to old age, but there's still more to follow... Even when we arrive in the world to come, there will still be more to follow.

"I see what you are saying, but what does this all mean for me?" I am so glad you asked. This means you do not ever exhaust the goodness, and the mercy, and the grace of our God. His goodness is without end. His mercy is without limitations. His grace is a characteristic of who He is. It's a part of His nature. He's unlimited. If it were just mercy, that would be amazing. How beautiful that mercy wipes out our sins as if they never happened!

But wait, there's more! I want you to know you cannot exhaust the goodness of our God. He doesn't leave us only washed whiter than snow, as mentioned in Psalm 51. He also brings us into His family. He calls us His children. God's grace and God's mercy fully revealed means that you have undeserved privilege.

But how can you be sure that His grace is for you?

For he raised us from the dead along with Christ and seated us with him in the heavenly realms because we are united with Christ Jesus. So God can point to us in all future ages as examples of the incredible wealth of his grace and kindness toward us, as shown in all he has done for us who are united with Christ Jesus. Ephesians 2:6-7

As you read this chapter, my biggest hope is that you gain a deep sense of peace. When we are weak, He is strong. When we fall short, He makes up the difference. Even when we stumble again and again in sin, God's grace abounds more and more. It's like beginning an ultra-marathon, but not being sure you've got what it takes to reach the distant finish line. God is saying to us, "Do what you can, bring your best, and I'll make up whatever you lack." As parents it can be our confidence that Proverbs 22:6 is true: "Train up a child in the way he should go, and when he is old, he will not depart from it" (KJV).

The truth is, we will never be perfect parents; we're all going to mess up, but God says, *"Do what you can, and I'll take care of the rest."*

PUT IT TO WORK

Our shortcomings are not news to God. All of us have blind spots. These might be areas you haven't yet identified where you haven't forgiven yourself.

Are there people you actively avoid because you feel ashamed or embarrassed?

Ask a friend that you trust to help you discover if there are any blind spots you need to uncover. A true friend will want to help you and won't use this as an opportunity to criticize things you can't change. Proverbs 27:6 says, "Wounds from a sincere friend are better than many kisses from an enemy. Was their input helpful and hopeful (enabling you to grow or just leaving you discouraged)?

Are you struggling to forgive yourself for sins that Jesus has covered? Write them down and leave them at the foot of the cross!

6

ENOUGH GRACE

What does your faith walk look like when the pressures of the world weigh heavy on you? This question isn't full of judgment. There is no right or wrong answer, but the answer does matter. There is something to be said about what your life looks like when you are holding all the burdens you can, maybe even a little more than you should, and life decides to hand you one more thing. I know this has happened to you before. In your mind as you read those words, you either revisited a moment of stress and seeming hopelessness, or . . . you thought about your situation right now. I'VE GOT GOOD NEWS! We aren't alone! The disciples knew that feeling too. Most everyone knows the story of Jesus walking on the water. That part alone can overshadow the amazing things that the disciples experienced in that story.

The disciples had been waiting for Jesus to return. When He didn't come back, they went onto the lake in a boat headed to Capernaum to look for Him. Patience wasn't really their strong suit, but it is so important that you see what happens when the disciples find themselves overwhelmed in a sudden storm. Look at John 6:16-18 in The Passion Translation. (I don't use the Passion Translation very often, but I love the way this passage reads.)

"After waiting until evening for Jesus to return, the disciples went down to the lake. But as darkness fell, he still hadn't returned, so the disciples got into a boat and headed across the lake to Capernaum. By now a strong wind began to blow and was stirring up the waters." (TPT)

By the way verse 19 in the New Living Translation says, *"A gale swept down upon them and the sea grew very rough."*

Now at this point, the disciples had more than they could handle. Their hands were full. With the boat being tossed side to side and water literally coming in with each crashing wave soaking them head to toe, they may have thought this was it. They weren't going to live to see Jesus again. Then something crazy happened.

The disciples had rowed about halfway (the NLT says 3-4 miles) across the lake when all of a sudden, they caught sight of Jesus walking on top of the waves, coming toward them. The disciples panicked (the NLT says "they were terrified"), but Jesus called out to them, "Don't be afraid. You know who I am." John 6:19-20 (TPT)

Why were they so terrified? Come on, we have all been here. You're doing all you can and then one more thing comes along, and that one more thing (sometimes) completely freaks us out. We get panicked and terrified because we don't know if we can make it with this "one more thing." The disciples' hands were so full, they were doing their best to stay afloat and make it across the lake. The waves are high, they're rowing against gale force winds; and then they see a figure walking towards them on top of the waves. Here's something interesting: When they see Jesus walking on the water, they revert to old superstition.

Let me share with you a piece of history that you may not know. In these times, it was believed that every storm had its own angry ghost. As Jesus was coming toward the disciples on the water, no doubt their fear and terror was caused by this old wives' tale coming back to (literally) haunt them in the present. This was *their* one more thing. They had their hands full already with the gale force winds and the waves threatening to over- take their little boat. They thought that death was upon them and now they had ghosts!

They were relieved to take him in, and the moment Jesus stepped into the boat, they were instantly transported to the other side! (v. 21)

Think about this for just a second. In all their travels, the dis- ciples got to experience Jesus doing miracles of healing the blind, the sick, and the lepers. He raised up the ones who were lame, and even brought a little girl back to life. This moment in the boat was a legitimate miracle too! I want you to see this and let it encourage you. Why? Because when we are in the middle of our own storms, God cares enough about us that He gets in our boats with us. We are NOT alone! Not only that, but He's going to get us to the other side. While we may not always be transported to the other side instantly, we will get to the other side much faster than we think.

By now, you know that I love to tell a good story, especially about my lovely wife, Hope. I am not proud of this story (except that I really, really am). This story begins when we were first married but I need to provide some context before I tell you the rest. I'll start by telling you that in the first couple of years after we were married, we developed a game between the two of us. One of us would jump out from behind doors or corners in our first little rent house and try to startle or scare the other. Who knows how these things get started (but in this case we DO know... it was totally my fault.) In the first decade of our marriage I loved jumping out and hearing her squeak in surprise. I scared her often and every once in a great while, she would get me back. However, in the following years a shift has happened that has been as unexpected as it is unwelcome. Somewhere along the way my sweet bride has developed stealth capabilities that cannot be explained! Her sneaking, stalking, and surprise tactics would make her the envy of any spy or ninja from a Hollywood movie! The tables have turned, and it has definitely NOT been in my favor. While that is true, I can always look back at this story with happiness. One of the first and still best scares happened like this... we were living in our first little rental house. One odd thing about the way this house was built was that the laundry room was on the complete opposite side of house from the bedrooms. Taking clothes out of the dryer meant that you had to walk from the laundry room, through the kitchen, through the living room, and down a long hallway to the bedrooms.

Why is that important to the story? Because I was sitting on the couch with Hope, and we had just finished sorting the laundry. The dryer's buzzer is going off and I know what is in the dryer: it's hang-up shirts. Now, let me frame this with the fact that we were young, and we didn't have kids yet. One of our two guest bedrooms had become our laundry room. We set up our ironing board and iron in place of furniture and the closet was where we hung up the shirts before we ironed them.

This means that I know what she is going to do: She is headed to the laundry room to get the "hang up" shirts that have to go in that closet. As soon as she gets up off the couch, I make a beeline for the room, turning off every light on my way to the closet and closing myself inside. Sure enough, about a minute later, here comes Hope. She has all she can carry, her hands are full, and she comes into the room. She has no hands to open the closet door. So, she uses her elbow to try to open the door and, just as she gets it open a little, she uses her toe to get it open the rest of the way. That's when I jump out and yell, "AHHHHHHH!"

Hope was not expecting it even a little bit! Her arms were overflowing with shirts and she was too startled to react. She just stood there, a silent scream on her face. After the shock wore off and the shirts fell to the floor I remember her taking a couple of quick swings at me and chasing me out of the room, both of us laughing till we couldn't breathe. While this is one of my favorite memories, it's also a great example of how easy it is for us to revert back to old ways of thinking. Hope knew it was just me in the closet, but that didn't stop fear from moving her to a place of inaction. Have you ever had a day when you already had your hands full? When you didn't need anything else added to your plate, yet out of nowhere you are startled with an unexpected challenge?

Now back to the story about Jesus walking on top of the waves to the disciples in the boat. The disciples had spent time with the literal Messiah yet, when they got caught in the storm with their hands full trying to row against the storm and they got handed one more thing, they fell prey to the old worldly superstitions about ghosts in storms and panicked instead of rejoicing that Jesus had come to rescue them.

Fear and panic can cause us to freeze up, unable to act. Has this happened to you? We, as Christians, have been told that we are living a blessed life. Don't get me wrong, we are! The problem is that we fall prey to the idea that it is supposed to be easy all the time. We get saved and we think, "Hey, now that I am following Jesus, I shouldn't have to go through anything hard." The truth is, sometimes, or even a lot of times, we are going to go through things that are hard. The struggle happens when we go back to that old way of thinking where we question if God is still with us, or if He is still for us. Like the disciples, we will all go through storms, and sometimes they are terrifying. But look at the difference when we invite Jesus into the boat with us. He helps us get to the other side! The important thing to remember is that the same God who is the God of the mountaintops is also the God of the valleys, and He will allow us to go through hard things. There's a big reason why that's true!

Let me remind you of Romans 8:28 where God tells us that He will work out everything for our good. I can hear you already.

If God wants to work everything out for my good, then why does He let bad things even happen?

If this question came to your mind, you aren't alone. It's a common question, but I want to answer it carefully and respectfully. In John 16:33 Jesus, speaking to His disciples, says, *"In this world you WILL have trouble. But take heart! I have overcome the world"* (NIV, emphasis mine). That's not the only place we find this kind of warning. First Peter 4:12 says, *"Dear friends, don't be surprised at the fiery trials you are going through, as if something strange were happening to you."*

If what we want is an easy life then we don't need God, we need a genie!

So, we can expect hard things and battles to come our way, but why?

We can rejoice, too, when we run into problems and trials, for we know that they help us develop endurance. And endurance develops strength of character, and character strengthens our confident hope of salvation. Romans 5:3-4

Consider it pure joy, my brothers and sisters, whenever you face trials of many kinds, because you know that the testing of your faith produces perseverance. Let perseverance finish its work so that you may be mature and complete, not lacking anything. James 1:2-4 (NIV)

Let me be really clear about this next statement; these passages of scripture don't mean that God CAUSED your pain, but if He allowed it, He loves you far too much to let that pain mean nothing! If what we want is an easy life, then we don't need God; we need a genie!

Now, the bad things, the horrible things, the things that break us, and make us look up and ask, "Why God?"—these are the things that ONLY God can take and truly make into things that could work out for the good of those who love Him.

When we are in the valley it is easy to feel as though we have been left alone to figure out our problems. This is when we must remind ourselves that the God of the mountaintops is also the God of the valleys. Instead, difficult times seem to short-circuit our brains, frozen only in the negative, but Psalm 46:1 says God is our refuge and strength, a very present help in trouble.

It's time for another story! The God of the valley never fails to show up, sometimes He just shows up differently than we expect.

What do you mean?

In the fall of 2005, I was riding my obnoxiously loud motorcycle with aftermarket exhaust pipes (yes, that's important to the story—you'll see why in just a minute) to a men's prayer breakfast at church. If my bike being ridiculously loud wasn't enough, add to it how difficult it would be NOT to see me because of all the shiny chrome and bright silver paint (again, important to the story—hold on a minute). After breakfast, as I headed home, I decided to swing by a shopping center where my friend, Leeroy, was leading the youth of the church in a car wash to fund their next youth mission trip.

They did a great job with all that chrome just shining as bright as it could! Leaving the car wash, I rode through the busy parking lot in front of a local grocery store to get out onto the main road. I was almost there . . . and that's when it happened. I wasn't speeding or riding recklessly. I was practicing all my defensive riding techniques, down the middle of a long lane out to the main road on my ridiculously loud and highly visible motorcycle, when I caught a flash of forest green from the corner of my left eye. In a split second it registered. *"Well, that there is a forest green Pontiac Grand Prix . . . and it's coming at me really, really fast. Does she not HEAR me? Does she not SEE me? How could she possibly miss me???"*

There was nothing to be done. I was about to be hit (remember that this realization is happening in my head at lightning quick speed). Reflexes took over and I tried to lift my left foot out of the way . . . I didn't make it. My last conscious thought was, "This is going to hurt." To be fair, I wasn't wrong.

Moments later, I woke up surrounded by what was left of my motorcycle—and her front bumper. She had fled the scene, and I was by myself in the middle of a crowded parking lot. Parked cars were on every side . . . but no people. *Had EVERYONE gone into the stores at the same time?* They must have, because there was not a single solitary witness to what had just happened. I remember being stunned and confused! The pain hadn't set in yet. I tried to stand to my feet but my left leg wasn't responding correctly. It was like my foot was out of sync. I looked down to see what was wrong and that's when it dawned on me . . . my foot was in the wrong place! It was BESIDE my shin, not where it belonged: UNDER my shin!

WHERE ARE ALL THE PEOPLE?!?

How was it possible that I was completely alone in a busy parking lot in the middle of a thriving suburb of Dallas, Texas. WHERE WERE ALL THE PEOPLE!?!

What seemed like forever passed (but it was truly only moments) and then a young teenager in a sedan drove by. I shouted as loudly as I could, and he looked my way. He literally did a double take, threw his car in park, and jumped out to help. He looked even more panicked than I felt. "What do I do, sir?" I asked him to drive down to the other end of the parking lot, where the teens were still doing the car wash, unaware of what had happened. "Go get Leeroy!"

I may have blacked out again, but it seemed like an instant later Leeroy was with me. He called for an ambulance and then I asked him to call my sweet bride (my phone was shattered). *"Don't talk to her! Just call her and then put me on the phone!"* Half a second later I was talking to Hope.

"Hey honey. Good news, bad news."

"What's up?"

"Well, the good news is that I'm okay, but the bad news is that I was hit on my motorcycle. The motorcycle is a total loss, and I know my leg is broken BUT I'm going to be okay."

"Are you SURE your leg is broken?

I looked down at my foot, which was obviously not in the right place. "Pretty sure (not telling her what my leg looked like). I'm going to have Leeroy take me to the hospital. Can you pick me up?"

She agreed, we hung up, then the ambulance arrived. I was trying my best to be brave and cool and joke with the paramedic and he was up for it until . . .

(In a suddenly serious tone) *"Mr. Angell, I'm not getting a pulse in your foot."*

(Me still trying to be funny) "I don't know how to feel about that."

"The blood flow to your foot has been interrupted."

"I don't know what that means."

"It means that if we don't get you to a hospital STAT so they can try to restore blood flow you could lose your foot."

(Me now matching his very serious tone) "Then get me in the ambulance and let's go!"

By the time I got to the hospital a group of the men from church had beat the ambulance there, were waiting for me, and praying. One of my friends was literally holding my hand while the doctors were working and assessing. They were able to restore blood flow and that's about the time the pain really hit in earnest. I told them (I thought rather bravely) to hold off on the pain meds because I wanted to look Hope in the eyes, and tell her everything was going to be okay. A short while later Hope was ushered into the room. I looked at her sternly and said, "Honey, everything is going to be okay!" As fast as you can blink, I looked at the doctor and said, "Okay, give me the drugs! He looked at me rather coolly and said, *"Sir, we've been giving you drugs."*

"I would like more please!"

They then told Hope that they were going to wheel me back to X-ray to assess just how much damage they were looking at, but that I'd be right back. As soon as I was out of the room, the doctor proceeded to explain to Hope that I was in shock (because I was still being upbeat and trying to be funny). Things WEREN'T going to be okay, and this was going to be a life-altering event as my ankle was shattered.

He went on to say that while I would PROBABLY be able to keep my wayward foot, I would probably never be able to put weight on it again, and we were going to have a long road to a recovery that probably included a cane or walker for the rest of my life. Hope told the men about the doctor's report, and they began praying HARD while I was still in the X-ray lab. I don't know how or when it happened, but something changed. I got back from the X-ray lab, the doctor received the X-rays of my foot and said, "Oh, this isn't nearly as bad as it looked." He updated his prognosis accordingly. "Okay, he will probably be able to walk on it again, though it will take at least two surgical procedures and a year of rehab. Limit your expectations; he won't be able to do anything athletic on that foot."

Hope went and updated the men. God had moved because the doctor was 100% certain that my ankle had been shattered, but now it was a simple break in the ankle and major tendon damage. The men got the report and, while it was much better, this news only fired up their fervency in prayer. They got back to praying and asked God to restore my ankle in full. An hour later they wheeled me into the operating room for the first procedure to stabilize the joint. It should have been a relatively short surgery; BUT it just so happened that the orthopedic surgeon on call was out and his replacement was an orthopedic surgeon that worked with the Dallas Stars Hockey organization (a specialist in this kind of thing).

> **God allows us to go through difficult things, but He has a reason.**

They kept me in surgery for several hours longer than anticipated; but in the end, they got everything done on the first try.

No follow-up surgeries, only two months in rehab, and while I have a couple of extra titanium parts, I also have complete use of my left foot. I run, play sports, and lift weights with no pain whatsoever.

What does all this mean? The God of the valley answers prayer even when the doctors don't know how or why! God didn't prevent me from being in an accident and experiencing the valley. Instead, He showed up IN the valley with me and changed the outcome to what HE wanted, versus the expectations of the doctors.

While there would be other battles to fight from this experience, I want you to see that only God can handle the difficult things with which we struggle—the things that set us back, the things that make us wonder, *Why is this happening?* And He can weave together something not just good, but beautiful, and strong, and powerful, and life-changing for you. It starts with you understanding and trusting that God's got this! It might not look okay, but if you trust in God, believing He's truly for you and that He never leaves you nor forsakes you, then these difficult things will work together for your good.

God allows us to go through difficult things, but He has a reason. Let's look at Romans 5:3-5 again, but this time from The Passion Translation. It says,

"Even in times of trouble, we have a joyful confidence knowing that our troubled times will develop in us patient endurance. Patient endurance will refine our character, and proven character will lead us back to hope. This hope is not as a disappointing fantasy; because we can now experience the endless love of God cascading into our hearts through the Holy Spirit who lives in us!" Romans 5:3-5

Let's go back and take a closer look. When we go through hard and difficult times these pressures will develop in us a patient endurance and that patient endurance refines our character. Then that proven character leads us back to hope. Before we move on, I need you to really see that this hope is not a disappointing fantasy. WHY?!? As you pass through the pain, even before you get to the other side you can still call on the endless love of God. He's still there. You aren't alone. Notice this! WHEN (not if) we go through hard things, if we'll be patient and endure, trusting that God has more than enough grace for us (even when it's hard), we will experience His endless love WHILE WE MAY STILL BE GOING THROUGH THE BATTLE! That tracks back to Psalm 26:1 where it says that He is our VERY PRESENT HELP in times of trouble. VERY PRESENT even when we feel like He is far off, because of what we're going through!

Grace doesn't mean that we'll never go through hard things because we will. It isn't a matter of if, but when. **Grace means that you will learn things in the valley you would never learn on the mountaintop!** It means that you will experience a dimension of His love for you that you couldn't experience in any another way.

PUT IT TO WORK

Our trust in God grows more in the valley than it does on the mountain tops. We also learn more about ourselves, the areas we need to grow in, and the grace of God in the hard times than we do when everything is good, comfortable, and easy.

What are some things you've learned in the valley?

How does your faith walk change when the pressures of the world weigh heavy on you? This question isn't full of judgment. It is to allow yourself the same grace that Christ has already given you!

Ask your heavenly, loving Father to show you how you can grow and learn in your battles rather than just asking for Him to make them stop.

What could God be showing you, or how could He be GROWING you in the middle of whatever battle you are in right now?

7

ENOUGH FORGIVENESS

"*New normal.*"

Does anyone else just hate that phrase? At the time of this writing, Covid and lockdown were still fresh and that phrase *new normal* was something we were hearing everywhere we went. What does *new normal* mean to you? To me it means things aren't the same and it insinuates that they will NEVER be the same. It implies that something has been lost and things will never be as good again. I heard that phrase after my motorcycle wreck. It meant that I would have to get used to pain in my ankle and loss of function, and it would have, but God . . .

Believe it or not, we can give purpose and new meaning to the phrase *new normal.* It doesn't have to mean something less, nor does it have to represent loss. Instead, it can mean growth and change for the better.

If we're going to experience growth and change for the better, there are some things we should leave behind. We must leave behind old hurts and old hang-ups. Our re-entry into normal is going to be entering into something *not less than,* but instead is *greater than*! This will represent growth and opportunity.

Let me ask you a question. Try to be honest with yourself, and trust me, I know that isn't always easy. What are you holding on to that you could leave behind? How about old wounds, battered emotions, and resentments? None of these things are ever going to serve you in a positive way. They hold you back from truly bringing all of yourself forward. How do we let go?

Now, it would be easy for me to say that the subject we are diving into is simple. After all, the Bible says we need to forgive . . . so there you go, but it is nerve-racking. The next step in our "More Than Enough Grace" is the grace to forgive. I am not even in the room with you, and I know it got quiet in your spirit. Maybe you're thinking, "I don't have any issues with forgiveness." Maybe you're reading this section and just praying for these poor people who are trapped in unforgiveness. Maybe you really ARE doing great, and you really aren't holding on to anything from your past. Or maybe you don't realize that you are. Most of us, whether we admit it or not, hear the term *forgiveness* and find that we are struggling with the topic of forgiveness because at any given time in our lives, we all tend to exist on one of two sides of the issue.

Maybe we have hurt someone and desperately want to be forgiven. I'm right there with you. Talking about forgiveness can make me uncomfortable. Why? It represents my own failures, my own mess up. At times I need forgiveness. Talking about forgiveness makes me uncomfortable because it brings back all the ways I've blown it, and how I need to repent and ask others and God for forgiveness.

Then there are those who are on the other side of forgiveness: the receiving side of hurt, still waiting for an apology that may never come. The side where we remain so caught up in something that was done to us, a way that we've been wronged, or an "unforgivable" hurt. We're not sure if we're ever going to be ready to let the pain and hurt go. Ask yourself why you'd want to hold on to the pain and just continue to live with it? We can struggle because forgiving them feels like we're saying what they did is okay. Like it didn't mean much of anything. Talking about forgiveness can tear open old scars we have spent our lives working to conceal.

I really love the C.S. Lewis quote that goes, ***"Everyone thinks forgiveness is a lovely idea until you have something to forgive."*** Think about that for a minute!

Time for another story!

Sometimes the easiest way to see the grace in forgiveness is when someone paints the picture for you. You're in luck because I have the perfect story about my teenage years, a tricked-out car, and my super excellent driving skills.

Were you an amazing driver when you were younger? Maybe you THOUGHT you were. Well, I really was! Why was I so sure? When I was 15 (without a license) I had an older (and licensed) friend, Joe, who had a really cool Ford Ltd. That baby was tricked out with chrome rims, chrome curb feelers, tinted windows, and a super plush interior. When we would go hang out together, didn't matter where we were going, he would toss me the keys and I would get to drive his car. Just to be clear, my parents did not know about any of this.

Joe said I was SUCH a good driver that he would let me borrow the car anytime I wanted. If I wanted to go see somebody or get a bite to eat or whatever, he would let me take his car. Now, I am sure you know that driving without a license is illegal, but I KNEW that I was *such a good driver* that I would never be caught. I believed that I was just as good a driver at 15 as anybody else on the road. My confidence at 15 years old was so high, I was driving the streets and highways of El Paso, Texas, with no supervision. At this age there is no realization of the danger I was putting myself and others in, nor the financial damages I could subject my family to if I had caused a wreck.

And then . . . one beautiful Tuesday morning at the corner of Cielo Vista Road and the I-10 Access Road in El Paso, Texas, I ran a red light. Honestly, it wasn't a really red light, it was more like a light pink, but the police officer that pulled me over disagreed.

He was merciful and kind enough not to impound the car, call my parents, and make a big scene. He was not, however, merciful enough *not* to give me a ticket. I drove away from the intersection with a ticket in my pocket and a deep sense of panic in my heart. Because I was an underage driver, I couldn't just pay the fine. Not only did I NOT have any money, but how was I going to appear in court before the judge, with my parents? How do I have this conversation?

When I got back to Joe's house, I gave him his keys and just spewed out what had happened. I was so scared I was sweating. It couldn't possibly get worse, right? Then Joe said, "Lafe, don't worry about it. I've got a plan. What you need to do is make sure to get the mail every day no matter what. That way when the notice comes in from the court you can intercept the letter, ask for a deferred court date, come up with a medical reason, and then forge your dad's signature."

That's a pretty good plan, right?

As if I hadn't already dug myself into a deep enough hole by driving around illegally, now I was digging it deeper. Joe's plan was just getting better and better. "You see, the officer who gave you the ticket must show up for court; and if they don't show up, the court will just waive the ticket. By the time you go in, he will have already been there several times so when it's your turn to appear before the court, the officer who wrote the ticket won't show."

Of course, that's not really the way it works, but that's what Joe said, and I had no reason to believe he wasn't right. With military precision, I watched the mail, intercepted the summons when it finally came, then sent back a request for deferment . . . and it worked! I deferred once, forged my dad's signature. I deferred twice, forged my dad's signature. Then it happened. I came home from school, happy as I could be because I've just had a good day. Everything's great, until I see my dad's truck in the driveway.

"That's odd, he's never home early."

Not only was he home early, but that also happened to be the day that he beat me to the mailbox. Another fun stroke of luck was that it also happened to be the day that round number three from the judge's office was waiting in the mailbox. But of course I didn't know that yet. Walking in the house, I see my dad sitting at the dining room table and I said something like, *"Hey, Dad, what's up?"* He didn't respond. I thought, *"That's weird!"* But then I looked at him. I realized he was not his usual smiling self. In fact, he was so angry that he was almost visibly shaking. I didn't know what was going on. It took me a moment, then I saw the seal of the court on the top of the paper he was holding.

"This is SOOO bad!"

In that moment, it's hard to describe the cold sweat and the sudden chill in the room.

It's also hard to describe what my dad meant by grounded. Grounded is one thing. But the type of "grounded" I met with that day was far beyond the realm of any normal grounding. Of course, I absolutely deserved all of that and more; and of course, there were some drastic reductions in my freedoms as a young teenager (most of which I could live with). But one decision threatened to ruin my life—or so it seemed to me at that age. When most kids would be getting their license at 16, I was now restricted to waiting to get mine until I was 17. With only two months till my 16th birthday, my license had been within arm's reach. As a 16-year-old boy (okay, okay, almost 16-year-old boy), my license was everything. Now, I was going to have to wait an extra year to get my license. This wasn't a court decision either; this was mandated by my parents.

As hard as that was, it was nothing compared to how I had hurt and betrayed the trust of my parents. There are times as a kid when you hear your mom and dad crying in their room, and you know it's because of you. That is the worst. So much worse than losing the ability to get my license for a year. Knowing that I had disappointed and hurt my parents, that I had lost their trust, was truly what hurt the most. In that moment I really wanted forgiveness and restoration. Not just on a surface level either, but on a deep level. And by the way, I had a great, great childhood. I had great teenage years. This wasn't the end of everything, but at that moment, it sure felt like it was!

Not knowing how to earn forgiveness and restoration, I just kept my head down, was profoundly obedient, and said I'm sorry for the hundredth time. Have you ever been there? Maybe that's you. When I say *forgiveness*, and it makes you uncomfortable, maybe it's because you're thinking about the ways you've blown it. Perhaps you've hurt people that you love and care for, or disappointed them. Maybe you're reading this part and you're thinking, *"I really don't want to talk about forgiveness."* Trust me, I understand! Maybe it's a painful subject because even though others have forgiven you, you haven't yet forgiven yourself. *"Yeah, but you don't know what I did."*

Maybe you're on the other side of forgiveness. Maybe when you read the chapter title you had a visceral response. In your mind, you automatically rushed to one of a couple of thoughts. Maybe your first thought was, *"But you don't know what they did to me."* Possibly you thought, *"But they've lied about me again and again."* There are a million reasons why we don't want to forgive. They wrecked your career on purpose. They fired you for no reason. Maybe you have been through so much that no one could even imagine the hell you have suffered.

Anger and pain are powerful emotions. Many of us who have been hurt struggle with thinking that they deserve to suffer the way they made us suffer. Maybe you're thinking, *"I'm going to make them pay."* Or maybe you're thinking, *"I will never, ever, ever forgive that person."* The problem with not forgiving somebody and holding on to old pains and hurts is that we begin to become inextricably tied to the person who has hurt us. We become connected to them just as surely as if we become their Siamese twin.

Our anger shapes our thoughts. It colors our future relationships, and it poisons everything we set out to do. We keep the person who has hurt us at the top of our minds. We could be having a really great day until somebody brings their name up. It is as if a dark cloud just floats over and begins to rain. Suddenly you're angry and wounded all over again.

"So can I forgive what seems to be unforgivable?"

"Why should I even WANT to forgive what seems to be unforgivable?"

If you're taking notes, I want you to write this down. If you're not taking notes, I still want you to write this down. Write it out on your arm, if necessary.

Why would we ever want to forgive something that we feel is unforgivable? It's because there are miracles on the other side of forgiveness.

Yes, there are miracles on the other side of forgiveness.

Yes, there are miracles on the other side of forgiveness.

Sometimes the things that hold us back in life, the things that cause us the most pain, the depression we can't seem to shake, the relationships that we can just never seem to make work, all have roots in unforgiveness. When we won't let go of past hurts, hang-ups, and the way somebody's treated us previously, everything about our future suffers. This pain, this state of unforgiveness, becomes your new normal. You get stuck in, *It can't get better than this. This is as good as it's ever going to be because you don't know what I've been through.*

So HOW do we forgive what seems to be unforgivable?

I am so glad you asked! Check out Ephesians 4:32. It says, "Instead, be kind to each other, tenderhearted, forgiving one another, just as God through Christ, has forgiven you." How about Matthew 6:14-15? It says, "If you forgive those who sin against you, your heavenly Father will forgive you. But if you refuse to forgive others, your Father will not forgive your sins." Now, that ought to give us chills if we really understand it.

Here's the deal. I know, on a daily basis, that I need God's forgiveness, His mercy, and His grace! I need it. I have to have it. The idea that God would withhold mercy and forgiveness from me because I've refused to forgive somebody else is terrifying. So, how do we do it? First and foremost, Jesus teaches us to pray for those who've hurt us. The very first words in Luke 6:27-28 are, "To you who are willing to listen." Just a sidenote: Not everyone is willing to listen!

Jesus teaches us to pray for those who've hurt us.

So before I take you any further into Luke, I just want to pray for you. *Father, today for everyone who's sitting here, book open in their laps, give them ears to hear. For the ones who have been bound up in unforgiveness, Father, I ask in Jesus' name, that you begin to loosen those shackles, Father God, help them to be <u>willing</u> to listen. In this moment, in Jesus' name, Amen.*

Verses 27 and 28 say,

"But to you who are willing to listen, I say, love your enemies. Do good to those who hate you. Bless those who curse you. Pray for those who hurt you."

Let me put this into historical context for you. I know, when we hear Jesus say something like this, most of us expect it. Right? Sweet, loving, and merciful. Jesus says, you need to love, forgive, and pray for those who've hurt you. Anyone in the Christian faith would expect Jesus to say something like that. But remember who Jesus is talking to. These are traditional Jewish people and Gentiles (Romans). His audience would have thought He'd lost his mind!

Why would the crowd of Jews be taken aback by Jesus telling them to forgive? Remember that they've been raised under the old covenant. The old Torah law, which by the way, calls for retribution. An eye for an eye, a tooth for a tooth, a life for a life. Sound familiar yet? They've been raised that this is what pleases God.

"Pray for those who've hurt you." In the King James translation, it says, *pray for those who spitefully used you.* The New Living

Translation says those who hate you. You pray for them. *What is He talking about? Has He lost his mind? That's not right.*

The Romans who heard Him say love your enemy, pray for those who spitefully use you, would have thought Him crazy as well. Why? Because revenge was such a big deal for Romans that they adopted and worshiped the Greek god of vengeance. Maybe you're smarter than I am, and you knew that already. But whether you knew that or not, it is fascinating what this god's name was. It was Nemesis. And, yes, that is exactly where we get our word *nemesis*. Nemesis is defined as a long-standing rival or an archenemy that causes your downfall.

When you allow somebody to become your nemesis, you are setting yourself up for a battle with no winners. They become a long-term rival or an archenemy that causes your downfall. Whenever you find yourself on a quest to get even, or maybe the desire for revenge is just in your heart, you must understand: If you persist on that path, you are worshiping Nemesis, not Jesus.

Okay, but how far can we take this? Surely there is a limit! There's something that somebody can do to us that is so bad, and so awful that we feel justified holding on to our unforgiveness toward them . . . And we even think it's okay with God because God understands how badly they hurt us. This justifies us in our unforgiveness that we feel toward them.

Joanna Weaver said, "Bitterness is like drinking poison and hoping the other person dies."

Then we look to Jesus. What does Jesus say about this? He said we must love our enemies. It's even more than that; we're instructed to pray for them.

Did somebody abuse you? Pray for them.

Did someone lie about you? Pray for them.

Did someone hurt someone you love? Pray for them.

Now this is where it hits home for me. You mess with me, we'll get past it. We'll figure it out. You hurt my wife or my kids, forget it. All bets are off. You become my nemesis. If you're a husband, a wife, or a parent, you probably understand how I feel. There are just some people and some situations that allow us to cross that line into wanting revenge. But when I allow that kind of thinking, I'm worshiping at the feet of Nemesis, not at the feet of Jesus.

If someone hurts someone you love, pray for them.

You know, the truth is if we're not careful, we find ourselves like Jonah. Jonah was sent on a mission to tell the Ninevites to repent. He didn't want them to repent. He became angry at God for wanting to show them mercy. And like Jonah, we can say things along the lines of "God, I don't want them set free. They should have to stay under bondage. They don't deserve your mercy." Can any one of us say that and believe it? If we're honest with ourselves, we don't deserve His mercy either. But if we'll follow Jesus in this, we're going to find that in moments like this, as we pray for someone who has hurt us, a prisoner is set free. That prisoner isn't the person who hurt us. The prisoner is you and me!

How do we, then, follow Jesus in this quest, this purpose to forgive? The truth is that when we're set free from bitterness and anger, we are then set free from the things that have hurt us. Isn't that the kind of freedom that Jesus has been fighting for in our lives since it began? Free from anger, free from bitterness, and free to experience the love and mercy and goodness of our God on a whole other level. That is real freedom!

Freedom to experience God's grace and mercy because God is more than enough. HIS grace is always more than enough when I fall short and I cannot forgive. Have you been in that space of unforgiveness—the hurt and pain of the wrongs committed that have had no retribution? If I'll give that thing to God, His "More Than Enough" grace to forgive will make up any shortfall I have in my own ability to forgive.

You might be thinking,*"This is just too hard. How am I supposed to let these hurts go? How do I forgive?"* If we are going to begin this journey of forgiveness, we are going to need a place to start. Let's make this practical. How do we do that? We pray. When we begin, we may have to pray through clenched teeth. I can promise you, you're not going to feel like it. That is normal. Just know, as the Holy Spirit begins to set you free through those clenched-teeth prayers, you're going to notice the softening of your heart.

If you will pray for those who hurt you, it will have change you for the better.

Let me add a disclaimer to praying for the people who've hurt us. When we pray for people who've hurt us, there's absolutely no guarantee that's going to change them. I've heard lots of stories about people who've prayed for their enemies and prayed for people who've hurt them, and they find out later that those prayers DID have an impact. That's awesome when it happens, but that isn't the endgame. There's no guarantee when you pray for somebody who's hurt you that it's going to have any impact on them. The statistic here that matters is that there is a 100% chance if you will pray for those who hurt you, it will change you for the better.

We become different when we pray those prayers. *How do I pray prayers that can impact my life this way?* We start by examining the attitude we have when praying for someone else. Chances are our attitude toward them is being impacted by the unforgiveness in our hearts. If we wait for the feeling, and if we wait to feel okay about it, we probably will never get there. We start by doing the right thing before we feel like it. We pray for the ones who've hurt us and we start here: *"God, do something."*

It's as simple as that. *God, do something.* God do what? We've left it open-ended. It gives Him space to move. If we are being real here, when we first pray that prayer it may have some edge to it. You know, "God, do something to 'em and smack 'em around a little bit. You know, make sure they know how bad they've hurt me, God, and show 'em how wrong they are." God knows your heart. It is no surprise to God if you feel this way. Start with, "God, do something." Start there.

What you're going to find is, as you are faithful to bring it before God, His "More Than Enough" grace to forgive will meet you where you are. If you're not strong enough to forgive, maybe you're not yet WILLING to forgive. No matter where you are in this journey, if you'll bring it to God and say, *"God, I need help with this. God, do something,"* He'll meet you in that place.

FORGIVE

"Forgive as you've been forgiven." Colossians 3:13 says, "Make allowance for each other's faults, and forgive anyone who offends you. Remember, the Lord forgave you, so you must forgive others." How do we forgive someone that we don't want to forgive? We forgive as the Lord forgave us.

What if the one who's hurt us is a family member? That makes things so much more complicated because we're between extremes. We're so angry at them, they should love us better and if they really loved us, how would they ever do (fill in the blank)? Maybe you're over on the other end and you feel guilty for having anger toward them. I want to make it more personal. And I apologize if this hits home. I'm not trying to hurt you, but I do want to set you free of the bonds that are holding you back from the freedom God is offering you.

It was Jesus Himself who said that adultery may be grounds for divorce, but adultery is also grounds for forgiveness. If you'll forgive, there are miracles on the other side of forgiveness. We forgive as we've been forgiven. Start here: *God, do something.* I have been here, where all I could say was: *"God, do something."* If you choose to forgive, it cannot change your past, but it will absolutely change your future. That isn't just a lofty promise. As you let go of things that have held you back and caused you pain, the shackles begin to fall off. You've been oppressed by these transgressions, so pressed down that you can't get free. We must be willing to forgive. Just being WILLING to forgive is power. That is your mustard seed of faith. You open the door for God to move when you are willing to forgive. When you forgive, it's not for them, it's for you.

God is looking to set a prisoner free, but it's not them. Yes, His heart is also for them, but He wants to set you free. James 2:12-13 says,

---

"So whatever you say and whatever you do, remember that you'll be judged by the law that sets you free. There'll be no mercy for those who have not shown mercy to others. But if you have been merciful, God will be merciful to you when he judges you" James 2:12-13.

First, can I just say that I am proud of you for making it this far. Forgiveness is not for the faint of heart. But it is for those who are ready for freedom. Jesus is the ultimate example of forgiveness. When each of us "took up our cross" to follow Him, we were prepared for the nice and sweet Jesus who says, "Love your neighbor but also love your enemy and pray for those who spitefully use you." As I said before, to the historical audience, this was crazy talk!

We also don't properly understand the gravity of the cross. It can be easy to think it was painful and hard. "God, I appreciate you doing that for me." Before we can understand why God expects us to forgive others, we must understand the gravity of what Christ went through to give us the freedom of forgiveness.

Before Jesus ever got to the cross, He was beaten. As a matter of fact, when the Roman officers went back to Pilate and said, "Hey listen, Jesus has passed away. Jesus is gone," Pilate's response was, "So soon, yet the thief on His right and the thief on His left are still alive?" Jesus didn't last as long as the others crucified beside Him because He had been beaten so badly. The prophet Isaiah told us in advance what was going to happen. He's going to be beaten so badly, they're going to strip the skin from His back. They're going to beat Him so badly that muscles and even some organs will be exposed.

Even without the cross, He probably would not have survived the beating He had already taken. When you're on a cross, the final cause of death is one of two things. One is a heart attack, the other is asphyxiation. Your lungs are slowly filling with fluid, making it more than hard to breathe. So when He speaks on the cross, He would have to push against the nails in His feet and pull on the nails in His hands to get high enough that He could open His chest up to get a breath of air. When He gets that breath of air, what He says is (and I am paraphrasing Luke 23:24), *"Father, forgive them. They don't even understand what they're doing."*

When I truly stop to think about what Christ went through so that I would not be lost, I'm overwhelmed. I'm blown away by that kind of mercy and forgiveness. They were actively killing Him, not just a quick and painless death, but in the worst way imaginable. Yet with all that pain, He stops and prays for the ones who are doing the killing. "I know these men are actively killing me right now, but Father, forgive them, they don't understand." Of course, they don't understand. They didn't know they were crucifying the Son of God, the creator of heaven and earth. The Living Embodiment of God made flesh, who was the one paying with His blood for the very sin they were committing against Him. He's dying on the cross to wipe the sin record clean. To give each of them a brand-new slate. If they had understood what they were doing, of course, they wouldn't have done it.

"Father, forgive them. They don't understand what they're doing."

When we stop to understand that the people who have hurt us, the people who have wounded us, did not understand what they were doing, our sight changes. *"How can you say that? You don't know what has happened to me. They meant to do what they did to me."*

Maybe. But what if they truly understood that they were hurting a child of God who was created in His image and is the apple of God's eye . . . priceless in His sight? Yeah. They would never, ever commit the sin that they committed against you. If any of us live long enough, we will for sure be hurt by somebody else. Some examples are the pain of abuse, gossip, unfaithfulness, mistreatment at work, maybe just a person who always seems to get on your nerves at work. It might even be that person who's always egging you on. Maybe it's the person who's always jabbing fun at you when you don't need it. Those tiny attacks begin to build up resentment toward them. Holding on to that aggravation is unforgiveness too.

Maybe this chapter about forgiveness has brought somebody into your mind, and you're saying, *"God, I don't know if I can."* Maybe these words have you thinking, *"I'm on the other side. I'm the one who's messed up so bad and they may have forgiven me, but I don't know that I can forgive myself."*

It could be that this chapter has brought to your mind feelings of anger at God. Can I tell you something? He already knows. It's not a surprise. What He wants most is for you to bring that to Him. He can set you free. He wants to take that anger and pain away from you. We might not understand until we get to heaven why things happened the way they did. But these things we know for certain: God loves us, He is for us, and if He has ever allowed pain in our life, He promises He will use it for our good (Romans 8:28). If you've been struggling with anger toward God, first off, He's not surprised and second, He's got big shoulders. He can handle it. If you are ready for freedom, you need to give it back to God.

PUT IT TO WORK

Forgiveness is one of the hardest topics to truly tackle, and even harder to put into action.

Are there areas of unforgiveness that you hadn't realized you're holding on to?

Are there any areas in your life where you just haven't been able to make any progress? Could this be because you've become anchored to a moment or event that wounded you and left you unable to move forward?

Is there a name that changes your mood for the worse when it pops up on social media? Could that indicate you've been holding on to a grudge? Based on this chapter, what will you do next if that's the case?

Pray for them. Remember, praying for them, isn't saying what they did is okay. Your prayer could even be asking God to lead you to a place to be able to pray for those you need to forgive. Even that is progress. Take that step and remember, even forgiveness starts small and leads to big change in your life!

8

ENOUGH HOPE

What does the word *hope* mean to you? No matter what your definition is, we can all agree that hope is a powerful word. It holds inside of it every possibility that can be when our hope is in the right place with the right motivation. What is hope, really? Is it, *I hope my family is safe on this trip?* Or *I hope that I get that big promotion so it can help take care of all my problems?* For hope to really make sense, we need to get to the heart of what it really means and for that we need to check out the book of Job. Now Job is a man who suffered immeasurable loss. In the matter of a day, he lost his entire livelihood, all of his children and was afflicted from the top of his head to the bottom of his feet with painful sores. He was a man well acquainted with suffering, and this verse hits it right on point. I won't make you read the whole passage but check out Job 8:13. It says, *"The hopes of the godless evaporate."* Let me repeat that. The hopes of the godless evaporate. If you're thinking that's a really weird way to kick this chapter off, you're not wrong. I just really want to

Godless hopes evaporate.

make a distinction here about hope. Let me say it differently to make myself very clear and maybe help you follow where I am going with this.

What if instead of saying, "The hopes of the godless evaporate," we say, "Godless hopes evaporate"? Godless hopes evaporate.

Have you ever said anything like, "I sure do hope the Texas Rangers win the World Series this year," or "I sure hope my wife says, 'Absolutely we should get that' about the cordless drill set that I want for Father's Day (wink, wink) from Lowe's"? What about, "I really hope that we have pizza for dinner tonight"? These are what I would consider godless hopes, and by the way, these hopes are not bad things. They are real hopes in our lives, but the truth of it is that they are centered around something other than God.

Let's go deeper with this. When we hope for things like this, it is because we believe they are going to make us happy in that moment. This type of hope doesn't require God to be involved. If the hope we're talking about doesn't cause us to lean further into Jesus and His presence, then it can become a godless hope. Before you start stressing out, I'm saying "godless"—not "ungodly"—hope because ungodly hopes are a whole different "thing" and it would be an entirely different chapter. We're talking about a godless hope, one that doesn't involve God at all—not a wish that is counter to God's Word or His purpose for us.

So, now that we have established what a godless hope is, let's bring in the last part of the verse in Job we were talking about. *Godless hopes evaporate.* Think about the things that you have been hoping for in your life, maybe you even have one of the hopes I listed earlier. Will you still remember you were hoping for those things in six months? How about in a year? In five years, or ten years? Will these "hopes" just be forgotten? If it isn't something you will remember pressing in on you in the future, then it was never a big deal. We hope for things that we believe will make us happy in a moment in time, but if they're not drawing us closer to God, they are godless hopes and they will evaporate.

What are "God-filled" hopes then? I can tell you one thing. They're not hopes for an easy life or for comfort or for all our problems to just go away. The kind of hopes that God gets excited about are when we hope to be used by God to make an impact in our world. When we hope to become what God has created for us to be. He's way more concerned about who we're becoming than what we do. He's way more concerned about how we're growing and maturing than He is about our happiness in a moment. We can think, "I'm doing godly things. I'm serving, I'm doing what I'm supposed to do." Those things are great, but God is way more concerned about the condition of our hearts than He is our list of accomplishments.

If God is going to grow us, use us, and mature us, if that's our hope, that's the kind of hope that God gets excited about. Throughout all these stories showing us how *God is More Than Enough,* we have seen so many different ways that God is more than enough for whatever comes next. And when I say more than enough "hope," I don't mean my wife, whose name is Hope; she's mine. You have to get your own. Let's just snuff out any confusion by the meaning of hope and lay down our biblical working definition of what hope means.

Hope is an eager, confident expectation that God is for us, that He has a purpose and a plan for our lives. Hope is an unwavering expectation that our loving God is working in every situation for our future. I didn't just make all of that up; it is straight from Romans 8:28, which says, *"And we know that God causes everything to work together for the good of those who love God and are called according to his purpose for them."* Let's just say that out loud. God works all things together **for the good of those who love Him and are called according to His purpose.**

Before you breathe that sigh of relief, I want to point out what it doesn't say. It doesn't say, *"God works all things together for those who just need more comfort in their lives."* It doesn't say, *"God works all things together for those who are just ready to be done with their struggles and problems."* It also doesn't say, *"God works all things for the good, for those who just want to be happy."* It says, "God works all things together for the good of those who love Him and are called according to His purpose." Let me tell you another story!

Before Covid, our kids had been begging us for a puppy for a while. With Hope and I being full-time pastors and with busy kid schedules on top of that, it was never a good time. Then Covid hit, social distancing started, and we found ourselves at home all the time. Out of nowhere it became an opportune time to get a puppy. When our daughter Noelle, came to us with the request, I was upfront with what we worried about from the start. "I know you're imagining all the wonderful things about having a puppy, like snuggles and puppy breath (that is gross . . .yet also cute at the same time) but you also have to be aware that there's a price that comes with this kind of responsibility." Despite the forewarning, she was committed, just as every 12-year-old is. "Dad, Mom, listen, I will take care of this dog. I've got this. It's not too much for me. I can handle it."

With sheer determination on her side, Noelle convinced us she could do it. When we got Trooper, he was nine weeks old and like any baby, he slept through the day and was up all night. Add to that the fact that he was leaving his litter mates for the first time when we brought him home. Noelle sets up his crate in the living room and gets him settled for bedtime. She puts him in his crate and soothes him until he falls asleep. Of course, I stay up late, listening for my dad cues, "Okay, are they settling down? Are they good? Okay, now I can go to bed."

I knew it would happen. A little after midnight, I hear Trooper start crying again. He had been quiet for a while, but he is in a new place and so he starts barking and howling that he wants out of his crate. I waited for Noelle to come in. Sure enough, didn't take long. When she saw me, she got a full sobbing cry going. "Dad, I'm just so tired and he won't go to sleep. What do I do?"

This is a defining moment as a parent, the opportunity to rescue or teach. What she wanted was for me to step in and take over. Instead, I had to say, "Baby, I hear you and I'm up right now because I want to be here for you. But understand, Trooper is okay. He's not hurt, or in any pain, he's just sad. What I need you to do is collect yourself. We can pray for Trooper but then you need to go take care of him yourself. If you need to, go make a little cot next to Trooper's crate and just put your hand on him and go to sleep. It's your job to calm him. You can't calm him if you are a mess."

Remember, she was convinced she was ready for this. Of course, if you asked Noelle today, she would tell you that it was all so worth it. But what about in those hard moments, at one o'clock in the morning when she's just so tired and the puppy won't go to sleep? Or if you ask her when the puppy is running around the house with her favorite stuffed animal, just ripping stitches left and right? If you ask her in those moments, is it still worth it? She might have to stop and wonder about it. There were still moments when she wanted to give up and ask, "Can you just take care of the dog?"

We must do the same kind of assessments in our lives when the hard moments come. We ask God, "I want you to use me. God, I want to be who you created me to be. God, grow me, mature me. God, I want to be all that you have for me to be." But guess what? There's a price for that. We think purpose and calling are free, but they come with a price. Isaiah 54:17 doesn't say that no weapon will be formed against you; it says no weapon that is formed against you will prosper.

We think purpose and calling are free, but they come with a price.

In John 16:33, Jesus says in this world we WILL have trouble, but we don't need to fear because He has already overcome the world. As you read this, really take a minute to understand that those God-filled hopes aren't going to come cheap or easy.

If you have your Bible sitting next to you as you read this chapter, I encourage you to go to 2 Corinthians 4:16-18. I am going to share the verse with you, but just take a moment to really hear in your spirit what this scripture is saying.

That is why we never give up. Though our bodies are dying, our spirits are being renewed every day. For our present troubles are small and won't last very long. Yet they produce for us a glory that vastly outweighs them and will last forever! So, we don't look at the troubles we can see now; rather, we fix our gaze on things that cannot be seen. For the things we see now will soon be gone, but the things we cannot see will last forever.

Just like the puppy, we have this list of benefits for living in God's purpose and a small list of what it will cost us. The problem is, when the cost comes, we begin to feel as though that benefit list has switched. What have you asked for in your life that now feels like the cost is too high, and the benefits don't feel worth it? What are the godly hopes that you've stuck out there? "God, I want to be more for you." But then the battles come, and we begin to weigh the scales. Is the benefit worth the cost? In the long term, of course the answer is going to be yes. But, at the moment? When you're in the middle of the battle, it doesn't feel easy.

OUR LIVING HOPE

When we see the Bible talking about our "living hope," we know that the Word is talking specifically about Jesus. We must understand that our hope is not just for ourselves and our relationship with Christ, but also for the world to come. A hope that's settled in your heart, that decision you made to follow Jesus. Now, let's talk about something that might make you angry because it goes against YEARS of modern American church tradition. Hopefully this isn't too scandalous, but just in case you didn't know, your salvation isn't based on a quick and easy prayer that you recited at a vacation Bible school years ago when you were eight years old.

A careful study of scripture will reveal that there is no prayer of salvation to be found in the Bible. Seriously, it doesn't exist. You can look for it all day long. You will not find it. You can find many prayers of repentance. If you read the Psalms, David was big on the prayer of repentance. He prayed prayers of repentance all the time. But I believe there is an unhealthy focus in many modern American religious traditions that if we get people to repeat after us, to just say the words, then they are saved. "Go about your lives as usual, you now have eternal hell insurance."

Romans 10:9 says that if you confess with our mouth the Lord Jesus AND believe in your heart that God has raised Him from the dead you will be saved. It's not one and done. The call that Jesus gave His disciples was not to pray a quick prayer, make sure you say it right, and then you're bound for heaven. No, what He said was, "Come, follow me."

So again, what are God-filled hopes? "God, I want to follow you. God, I want you to use me. God, I want to become what you have planned for me to become. I want to accomplish the things you have in mind for me. If I was born for such a time as this, before I was ever born, you had a purpose and a plan for my life. You wanted to use me in your kingdom and use me to reach nations and people, to touch lives with hope, with confidence that our God is good, and that He is for us and not against us! Let me be filled with THAT kind of hope."

"You're going to be fighting some battles; but fear not, I've already overcome the world" (paraphrased). We can't let go of our godly hopes. Go ahead and let go of the ungodly and godless hopes but hold on to your God-filled hopes.

I've tried to pray my problems away like everyone else, and there are times when I face trials and battles and ask, "God, can you just take this away from me?" Sometimes He will, and that's great. However, there will be times where there is a lesson to be learned in those troubles, or strength to be gained, and we need to be prepared to walk through it with God.

To be clear, I am by no means asking you to just grin and bear it. We should always ask God about our troubles and bring them before Him because as you've heard me say before, when we bring God the things that cause us anxiety and struggle, He takes our anxiety and gives us peace in its place.

Don't worry about anything; instead, pray about every-thing. Tell God what you need, and thank him for all he has done. Then you will experience God's peace, which exceeds anything we can understand. His peace will guard your hearts and minds as you live in Christ Jesus. (Philippians 4:6-7)

Then in verse 8 He tells you how to keep that peace.

And now, dear brothers and sisters, one final thing. Fix your thoughts on what is true, and honorable, and right, and pure, and lovely, and admirable. Think about things that are excellent and worthy of praise. (This is an incredibly import-ant principle that I'll talk more about in the next chapter.)

Let's just debunk the myth now that if you're blessed you don't have struggles. And if you have struggles, then you're not really blessed. You can, in fact, be both blessed and still have struggles that you're walking through. I can pray for God to take away my struggles, for Him to free me of my issues and the things that are causing me unrest and anxiety. You know what? God is not interested in an easy life for us. He's not interested in making it comfortable for us. He knows that an easy life full of comfort is not going to help us reach His best and highest purpose for our lives.

"So, what does *More than Enough Hope* really mean?" First of all, it doesn't mean, "I have hope that we will make it through this." That may be a hope, but it isn't the "More than Enough" Hope that God wants us to have.

God wants to grow and mature us. That means our hope is not measured by our desire for an easy life. Our hope instead is to live a life that honors God and is effective in expanding His kingdom in the lives of the people we touch.

Hebrews 6:17-20 says, "God also bound himself with an oath, so that those who received the promise could perfectly be sure that he would never change his mind." So God has given both His promise and His oath. These two things are unchangeable because it is impossible for God to lie. Therefore, we who have fled to him for refuge can have great confidence, have great hope. We can have great confidence as we hold on to our hope with all that lies before us. The kind of confident expectation of good because of the promises of God. This hope is a strong and trustworthy anchor for our souls. It leads us through the curtain into God's inner sanctuary.

Often, we know that God has come through for us in the past, but we hit the next speedbump and think that He has left us alone to figure out the problem we are facing. There is no better place to see how easy it is for us to forget what God has done than Moses in Exodus. Have you ever read the story of Moses and the Israelites? One of the most well-known stories in the Bible is about him. Moses brought God's people, the Israelites, out of Egypt. Throughout their journey from slavery to freedom the Israelites complained. They heard God speak! Imagine for a moment hearing your Creator speak to you. Miracle after miracle was witnessed and yet the Israelites complained every time things got tough AND they had enough.

I can get so frustrated reading the stories. "God just split the Red Sea for them! He just took out the entire Egyptian army to protect them! Then they get a little hungry and start complaining against God?!? That's a lot of nerve!"

But the truth is we do the same thing. God did not rescue us in our past to abandon us here in the middle of this battle. "He who began a good work in you will carry it on to completion" (Philippians 1:6 NIV). Despite this promise, we forget that. Why? Because sometimes we're going through stuff, and it seems like wave after wave after wave that just won't quit. The God who rescued you in the past will not suddenly forget you. The Israelites certainly gave God plenty of reasons to WANT to forget them by continually complaining. Why did He continue to rescue them? Because God doesn't change.

The God who rescued you in the past will not suddenly forget you.

The same God who rescued them in the past provides a confident expectation that He's going to rescue them again and again! When there's a need, He will lead, guide, direct, provide, restore, heal, and defend His children. He always does. Yes, we can have a confident expectation in our hope; because we have a track record to look back on to see our God, and how He has been good to us. If we're honest in this moment, every single one of us has a reason to say, "Okay, I'm amazed I made it this far."

I'm going to remind you of the three things that try to steal your hope: Number one, negative voices in your life. Number two, bad alignments. Number three, self-pity. Self-pity is the enemy of all your hopes and dreams. The enemy's out to steal and rob your hope. To leave you feeling hopeless. To not lose hope, we can trust that ours is a God of mercy, grace, and love. We can trust that if He allows suffering or trials, He will absolutely 100% of the time use it for good in our lives. He cares about us way too much to let any of the things we go through be wasted.

I pray that God, the source of hope, will fill you completely with joy and peace because you trust in him. Then you will overflow with confident hope through the power of the Holy Spirit. (Romans 15:13)

Maybe, as you read this chapter, you are reflecting on the challenges and the seasons in your life. It can seem easier sometimes to just sit in silence than take a stand. Maybe you've thought, "At least if I am silent, I won't be singled out for attack." When you step out in faith and accept God's hope, the enemy might cause trouble and temptation to come in like a flood. Those waves could possibly sweep you off your feet and bring dismay and destruction.

With all these fears, why would anyone want to be a part of what God is doing? Let me provide you with a blessed assurance. The enemy is already defeated! No weapon formed against you will prosper. That doesn't mean no weapon will be formed, it just means that no weapon formed against you will prosper! When the enemy comes in like a flood, God raises up a standard. You are that standard. God is raising up the church as the standard. The world is telling you why you should be scared, but our hope in our God tells us that in Him we can stand. We, as the church, the people of God, should be the standard that God is raising up in this hour. When the church is raised up, none of us stands alone. At times we may struggle and our hope might waver. When that happens the church of believers should be there to stand in the gap.

"It just seems like more is going wrong than we've ever seen go wrong before!" God put you on the earth in this season on purpose, in this moment, this hour, "for such a time as this"! Yes, we were not born by mistake in this season. It cannot be repeated enough that no matter the trials and pain we face, no weapon formed against us will prosper.

We could say, "That sounds all warm and fuzzy, but in my life right now in this season . . . I'm being shaken and I feel like pieces are falling off of me. I don't know how to grab onto that promise."

Let the shaking happen! What falls away was not meant to be there. What's left is holy, purified, proven, and true. God will do more with what's left after the shaking than you could ever imagine. As you read these words, I can almost hear you thinking, "How can I be sure? How do I have hope when I've lost so much?" Dear reader, I am praying for you right now. For strength to hold on and wait. Listen, not only are you going to come back from this, but if you'll let what can be shaken off fall away, what's left will be purified and proven wholly true. Yes, God will use what little may seem to be left, to do way more than you ever imagined possible in your life, and in the lives of those you touch and bless.

YOU were created to bear His image in the world and bring hope and salvation.

For such a time as this, with purpose and joy, YOU were created to bear His image in the world and bring hope and salvation. You may not be able to impact the whole world, but you can and WILL impact the world of the people He sends you to. Your path is charted like an arrow from His bow. God wants to send you right to the ones who need Him! He wants you to proclaim His goodness, His mercy, and His grace. You are the voice of victory in somebody else's life.

Do you think for a moment that God's going to let you fail? No. The enemy is a defeated foe. You're created for such a time as this! You're in the plan of God's kingdom. You are the standard of hope and joy that He is raising. And by the way (and this is a BIG ONE) you're going to win. *You're going to win.* Give it to God. Pick up the hope and joy that He is providing for you, and you will win. The storm may be rolling in, the wind may be blowing, the seas may be rough, but keep your eyes on Jesus. Remember that you are the standard, and that you are made to win.

PUT IT TO WORK

What kind of "hopes" are filling your mind? Do your hopes lead you further on in faith or are they more for your own temporary happiness?

Knowing what "God-less hopes" are and what "God-filled hopes" are, how will you change your focus on what you truly hope for?

What NEW hopes will you walk in with your new focus on God-filled hopes?

ENOUGH

9

ENOUGH PEACE

"The peace that surpasses all understanding . . ." How many times have we heard this verse and wondered, *How do I get there?* The best way for us to jump into the topic of peace is to start with Philippians 4:4-8. Get comfortable; we're going to camp out here for a while. Let me walk through it with you beginning in verse 4.

Rejoice in the Lord always. I will say it again: Rejoice! (NIV)

You and I just need to pause for a moment as you read this because rejoice is emphatic! That's not if you feel like rejoicing or if you are in the mood. This is a direct command. The apostle Paul is saying rejoice. He doesn't say, depending on your circumstance, if everything's working out, if you're feeling good, if you got a raise, if your kids are behaving, if the dog didn't make any messes in the house this week, then rejoice. No, just rejoice. Rejoice in the Lord always, I will say it again, rejoice!

> *Let your gentleness be evident to all.* ***The Lord is near.*** *⁶Do not be anxious about anything, but in every situation, by prayer and petition, with thanksgiving, present your requests to God (emphasis mine).*

Verse 6 says be anxious for NOTHING! Really, this must be some kind of biblical prank, right?? Clearly Paul didn't know about Covid, economic crashes, or elections. He has never sat in traffic trying to get safely home. Don't get me wrong, Paul lived in a world where LEPROSY was still a real thing you had to be worried about. (That was the ultimate social distancing.) Not to mention religious persecution, government executions by LOTS of different methodologies. If you could die by it, there was a chance that someone was using it as one of their ways to execute you.

How is it even possible not to be anxious about ANYTHING? Paul gives us the alternative for anxiousness. In EVERY situation take your concerns to God in prayer, and as you do, remember who you're praying to. Pray with thanksgiving and mindfulness of how good and faithful God has been in your story. He has blotted out your sins and has chosen to forget them. He paid the highest price imaginable to give you health and peace. Think too of all the ways, both seen and unseen, in which He has protected you and provided for you. We have a lot to be thankful for and an unshakable confidence that "He who began the good work in you will be faithful to complete it."

Now back to Philippians 4:6-8.

Next up:

And the peace of God, which transcends all understanding, will guard your hearts and your minds in Christ Jesus.

He promises us peace that is beyond our understanding, but for what purpose? To guard our heart and mind, but in the flurry of life, we just don't get it. You don't just automatically get peace. You only get the peace that is promised in verse 7 if you go through verse 6 first. Be anxious for nothing, but in everything with prayer, petition, and thanksgiving, make your requests known to God! **And then**, He will give you His peace that passes understanding to guard your heart and mind.

I don't know about you, but I am prone pray to God, take my needs to God, lay them down at the feet of Jesus, and then promptly take them back. When we pray and say, *"God, I need help with this area, I'm turning this over to you,"* the last thing we should do once we finish praying is begin worrying! "What if He doesn't answer my prayer?" In essence, that is taking your concerns and the things that make you anxious back off His lap and holding on to them yourself. We must stop using the things that give us those anxious feelings like a strange security blanket! Let me ASSURE you, I've done this too many times to count. You are not alone in taking back the things you have tried to entrust to God.

We must stop using the things that give us those anxious feelings like a strange security blanket!

"God, I trust you with this, but let me take that back for a minute and worry over it some more." Once you've given it to God on the altar of prayer, LEAVE IT THERE!

But how? Let's touch on that for a moment. *What if it doesn't work out the way I think it needs to work out?* That is where verse 8 comes in. The instructions on how to stay in the peace He gives you are:

Finally, brothers and sisters, whatever is true, whatever is noble, whatever is right, whatever is pure, whatever is lovely, whatever is admirable—if anything is excellent or praise-worthy—think about such things.

Don't allow yourself to dwell and worry about the things you've entrusted to God. Instead, think about things that will encourage and build your faith. This passage has been taught (countless times) in the same way we look at the proverbs, as if it were a collection of separate ideas and wisdom. The problem with that is you CAN'T look at it that way! When someone gives you an instruction manual to repair a car, you don't pick and choose in which order to do each step. You start with the first step and work your way through. It is the same with Paul's instructions for peace. Your instruction manual begins in verse 6. Don't be anxious; pray with confidence and thanksgiving. Verse seven BEGINS with the word *And*. You don't get verse 7 without verse 6. Verse 8 begins with the word *Finally*. We might say, "One more thing." Verse 8 tells us how to stay in the peace we were given in verse 7 that came when we prayed in verse 6! When you feel yourself begin to worry and become anxious, stop yourself right there in that moment, go back to verse 6, and repeat the process.

"God, I feel myself becoming anxious again so one more time I give you control of the things I can't do on my own. You've been so good to me, and I KNOW I can trust you in this moment.

"Thank you for your peace that you pour out over me, a peace that only you can give no matter the size of the storm. I ask that you cause your peace to guard my heart and mind to keep me steady and strong in you.

"Finally, I will choose to meditate on your goodness and all of the things that you've done in my story. I will remind myself of who you are, who I am in you, and why I am so confident."

Your peace is not dependent on your circumstance.

Your peace is **not** dependent on your circumstance. It IS dependent on your prayer life and the promises of God.

In John 14:25-27, Jesus says, *"These things I have spoken to you while being present with you. But the Helper, the Holy Spirit, whom the Father will send in My name, He will teach you all things, and bring to your remembrance all things that I said to you. Peace I leave with you, My peace I give to you; not as the world gives do I give to you. Let not your heart be troubled, neither let it be afraid." (NKJV)*

The Passion Translation says this verse a little differently, and I want you to hear Jesus in these words:

"I leave the gift of peace with you—my peace. Not the kind of fragile peace given by the world, but my perfect peace. Don't yield to fear or be troubled in your hearts—instead, be courageous!" (v. 27)

So, what's the point? The peace we're looking for doesn't come from people, so people can't take it away, UNLESS we let them. The peace we're looking for doesn't come from our circumstance; so if our circumstances change, our peace is not suddenly in doubt.

No better story to share with you about keeping peace in the middle of peril than Daniel and the lions' den found in Daniel 6. Daniel spent his whole life serving God but living in the world's politics. Despite that, he always brought the kingdom of God wherever he went. When a new king came along and took over, Daniel continued to work with excellence. Unfortunately, there were other officials who were jealous of Daniel and his position of authority and respect. Since they couldn't find any fault in him, the administrators and high officers attacked Daniel's faith. Have you ever had someone use your faith as a weapon against you?

The administrators and high officers had a plan. They went to the king and convinced him to create a law that would have anyone found praying to any other god (other than the king) be thrown into a lions' den. They told the king, "All the king's advisors and governors agree that the king should issue this law." They lied because Daniel, who was one of those advisors, certainly didn't agree! After the king agreed and enacted the law, they told the king, "That man Daniel, one of the captives from Judah." First, notice they not only left out his title, but they changed it. Daniel the captive. They didn't say, "Your second in command in all the kingdom," or "Daniel the wise one who's running your affairs so well that there's nothing to criticize." What they said was: **"Daniel, one of the captives."**

If you allow the enemy, he'll redefine you as a captive.

"That man Daniel, one of the captives from Judah, is ignoring you and your law. He still prays to his God three times a day." Listen, King Darius was a smart guy, and just hearing about this, he knew he got played. How do we know this? In 6:14, he said,

"Hearing this, the king was deeply troubled, and he tried to think of a way to save Daniel. He spent the rest of the day

> *looking for a way to get Daniel out of this death sentence; but in Babylon, not even the king could change the law. The king gave orders for Daniel to be arrested and thrown into the den of lions. The king said to him, "May your God, whom you serve so faithfully, rescue you."*

Listen, Daniel was so characterized by the peace and grace of God that a man of the world, a king who had no connection to God except through him, said, "Hey, I am rooting for you. May the God you serve so faithfully rescue you." *What happened next?* Something amazing! The king returned to his palace and spent the night fasting. He refused his usual entertainment and could not sleep at all that night. Very early the next morning the king got up and hurried out to the lions' den. When he got there, he called out in anguish, "Daniel, servant of the living God!" (His language has already changed.) "Daniel, servant of the living God! Was your God, whom you serve so faithfully, able to rescue you from the lions?"

How do you think Daniel responded? Well, I can tell you what he didn't say!

"Yeah, but one of them was looking at me funny. Please get me out of here."

He didn't say:

"Yeah, but all night long this one's been scooching up closer and closer to me, and he's drooling. Can you please get me out, like now?"

Instead of what would be expected from someone who spent the night waiting to be the lions' dinner, Daniel answered in peace. "Long live the king! My God sent the angels to shut the lions' mouths so that they would not hurt me. For I have been found innocent in his sight and I have not wronged you, Your Majesty."

The king was overjoyed and ordered that Daniel be lifted from the den. Everyone there looked on in surprise as there was not a scratch to be found on him. Why? He had trusted in God. Even better (I love this part!), "Then King Darius sent this message to the people of every race and nation

> **No matter the trials you are facing, peace is always there for the taking.**

and language throughout the world: "Peace and prosperity to you! I decree that everyone throughout my kingdom should tremble with fear before the God of Daniel. For he is the living God, and he will endure forever. His kingdom will never be destroyed, and His rule will never end. He rescues and saves his people. He performs miraculous signs and wonders in the heavens and on the earth. He has rescued Daniel from the power of the lions."

Let me tell you that when you live your faith out loud, the way it was intended, others can see it and hear it in you! No matter the trials you are facing, peace is always there for the taking. We simply trust God has our back and we keep going. When the world sees that you simply cannot be broken because of your faith, that is when your example has the chance to change the world. The very character of Daniel was on display. Look at what Daniel's faith did; it rescued him from the lions' den; but even more, his faith showed a king who did not know God for himself, WHO God is!

Daniel was at such peace that even the lions became calm. Like Daniel, we have opportunities to experience encounters with God, but sometimes those encounters with God come in uncomfortable situations and circumstances. Can we still have peace to emerge from a terribly hurtful situation? Can we be like Daniel? We need to have the peace he showed to people of the world! Kings and leaders alike saw the testimonies to God and what He was doing in Daniel's life. Let us work to be like Daniel, going through trials and struggles from a place of peace, being convinced of the power, authority, goodness, and faithfulness of our God, showing others like King Darius, how powerful our God is, by the peace they see in us.

FEAR, WORRY, AND THE UNKNOWN

What is your prayer life like? For Daniel, his peace was born out of his prayer life. Far too often, we allow ourselves to be shaken up by the concept of prayer. Why do we overcomplicate speaking with God? Well, in many cases, the church has made prayer into a super spiritual, highly technical, highly skilled activity that only certain believers are really good at.

It happens to each of us in our faith journey that speaking a prayer out loud becomes a bit of a stage fear. We compare our prayer life to that one person that you probably know. No matter what the occasion is, or what he's asked to pray for, he's going to pray a really long, impressive, theologically sound, timeless, and yet relevant, super impressive prayer. He's going to cite five or six scripture verses (verbatim) and unite them into the need at hand.

He may be amazing at prayer but, man, you don't want him to be the one that prays for Thanksgiving dinner! "No way, Bob can't pray for Thanksgiving this year. Remember last year? Yeah, I don't want to wait a week to eat." The other part of this is the insecurity about our own prayer life when we hear others pray. "Well, he's got a stronger prayer life than me." Why? "Man, when he prays, it just sounds so impressive. I don't sound like that."

Add insult to injury, 1 Thessalonians 5:16-17 tells us to pray without ceasing. WHAT?!? That is super overwhelming because who has that kind of time? Who has that much to pray for? Or that many words! When we allow the enemy to make us feel like failures at prayer, we open the door to losing our peace. Why? We fail to take anything to God in prayer. It feels like we're praying to an English professor (an old senior English professor) at a great distance. Then, when we do decide to pray, we feel like God is evaluating our effort in prayer. He's going to mark it wrong with a big red Sharpie if we don't have enough scripture references. Heaven forbid incorrectly citing a scripture reference in the midst of prayer or using poor grammar in your prayer. God is only going to answer the prayers that are impressive to listen to.

If you have ever been made to feel this way, let me just say, I'm sorry. Prayer truly is just about the intimate relationship between you and God. It simply isn't true that there is a wrong way to pray. Prayer does not have to be complex or hard. Talk to Jesus in your everyday moments and enjoy authentically sharing what is on your heart. This kind of prayer is what God is seeking. Remember that verse in 1 Thessalonians? When Paul says pray without ceasing, it is in the context of a conversation, not a monologue.

THE SPIRIT OF GRATITUDE

What does gratitude have to do with having peace? Well, I can have peace amid distress because our God is faithful. When you and I give thanks in our struggles, it puts us in the middle of the will of God. "In everything give thanks; for this is the will of God for you in Christ Jesus" (1 Thessalonians 5:18 NASB). How do we know for sure we're in the will of God? We can know it when we give God praise and thanks through everything—the good and the bad stuff. When we're in the midst of all that, and we can still find a way to say we are "blessed" when we are "struggling," then we are in the middle of the will of God. When are you out of the will of God? It doesn't matter how blessed you are, if you're somebody who grumbles, complains, and gripes, guess what? Before you close the book, I am just calling an orange an orange.

We must cultivate a spirit of gratitude. Gratitude isn't just something some people get. It is just like building muscle. If you're always complaining, always griping, then it becomes natural. This bad habit has now become second nature. The good news is you can turn that around. Yes, I will choose to praise God in the middle of my situations. If I'm sick, He is my healer. If I'm broke, He's my provider. If I'm struggling, He's my peace. In the midst of my difficult situations, I will sing out loud and praise the name of God. David says, "I'll praise God seven times a day" (Psalm 119:164). If we cultivate a heart of gratitude, then we get to walk in peace. The chains fall off and bars of iron are broken. He brings us into harbors on calm seas.

Wait, how do we get that peace again? Oh yeah, give God thanks first, and keep giving Him thanks along the way.

Wait, sometimes things are too hard; how can I walk in peace if my world is falling apart? Choose to praise God in the middle of everything all the time, without exception, even (and especially) when it's not going the way you want. Even when sometimes it hurts, praise God in the middle of everything. Giving thanks puts you right in the middle of the will of God. As a matter of fact, when Jesus is facing 5,000 people who are all hungry and they hand Him a boy's lunch, five loaves and two fish, what is the very first thing He does?

He gives thanks for these five loaves and two fish. If you know this story, you know that wasn't enough food to feed 50 people let alone 5,000. Still, Christ gives thanks. He knows what God's about to do. Even when you feel like it's not what you need, even when you feel like it's not enough. Because God can do amazing things from small beginnings, one thankful word of praise at a time. The more praise we speak, the less room there is for the negative voices that rob us of peace. Peace starts with thankfulness.

Have you ever heard the song, "It Is Well with My Soul"? It is a song that I love, and it is a perfect example of giving thanks in all things. When Horatio Spafford wrote those famous words, he was on a ship. His wife and four daughters had been traveling ahead of him on another ship, the *Ville du Havre*. Without warning, their ship crashed into an iron hulled Scottish ship, the *Loch Earn*. Within 12 minutes, the *Ville du Havre* went down, taking Horatio's four daughters with it. A small fishing vessel rowing through the wreckage happened to see a woman floating on a piece of what once the ship and rescued her. It was Horatio's wife. Once on dry land, his wife sent him a telegram about what had happened.

That is why he found himself on a ship, passing the exact spot where his daughters' ship had been lost. In those moments, he writes the words, "When peace like a river attendeth my way, when sorrows like sea billows roll, whatever my lot, thou hast taught me to say; it is well, it is well with my soul."

Listen, it is no accident that you are reading this book right now. Romans 8:1-39 (I know its long, but it's important) tells us that no matter what you've been through, no matter how many ways we've blown it, no matter how many burdens we're carrying with us, there's no condemnation. There's no comparison. Even when we're walking with God we can still mess up. Thankfully, every time we mess up He will bring us back into the fold. Mistakes are what make us human. Despite our nature and the flaws that so define our humanity, with God there is no separation, no condemnation, and no comparison.

The Apostle Paul in the Book of Romans says, (my paraphrase) *"The same God, who is for you, who predestined you, who called you and now has justified you, has also glorified you"* (Romans 8:30). Paul was so sure about this that He spoke about it in the past tense; it has already been accomplished. Why? Because of the goodness of our God. Before we can have that "More Than Enough" kind of peace, we must believe that with God, through Christ, there is no separation, no condemnation, and no comparison.

When I say peace, I'm not talking about a little peace. I'm not talking about *I'm a little stressed, but mostly I'm okay* kind of peace. If you could take away anything from this chapter, I want you to understand how you can walk in the path of peace, even in difficult times. Number one, we're going to give thanks to God in everything, for this is the will of God in Christ Jesus for you. I want to stay in the middle of His will, so I better get really good at thanking my God all the time. And I can have confidence because my assurance is not in my own strength. If it was, I could never be confident.

My confidence is rooted and grounded in the fact that my God is more than enough, is faithful, and loves me. Augustine said it this way, "God loves each of us as if there were only one of us." Let me say that a little stronger: God loves you as if you're the only one here. He loves you as if you were the only one to love. He so loves you, that He would've paid the price that He paid for all of us, just for you. That is powerful. Grasping at peace can be difficult sometimes, but one thing is certain, God so loves you. He loves you like you are His only child, and because we are His . . . we have more than enough peace.

PUT IT TO WORK

We took a lot of time on Philippians 4:6-8 in this chapter. Verse 7 says THEN He will give you peace… and that peace has a purpose! That peace is supposed to guard your heart and mind, but you don't get the peace in verse 7 without going through verse 6 and giving the things that make you anxious to God WITH THANKSGIVING (praise). There's a similar instruction in Psalm 100:4, "Enter into his gates with thanksgiving, and into his courts with praise." Praise is connected to gratitude and gratitude is connected to peace. That means your peace is directly connected to your praise and worship life.

Do you struggle to have peace?

If you find you are short on peace, remember that Paul said to rejoice!

What can you be grateful for today?

Have you expressed that to God in prayer or worship?

_____

_____

_____

_____

_____

_____

_____

_____

_____

_____

_____

_____

_____

_____

_____

_____

_____

_____

_____

_____

_____

_____

_____

_____

10

ENOUGH LIGHT

Have you ever found yourself stumbling in the dark? The flashlight dimmed and the batteries finally failed. And there you are in the attic, basement, or someplace unfamiliar. You stand completely still not knowing what to do next. Or maybe you choose to be brave and begin to fumble your way around. Without light it is hard to complete even the simplest tasks. We can easily take for granted what is so readily available. Even in familiar settings (think about walking through your house at night with the lights off), you know where you are, you know where everything is, but then there's sometimes an unexpected noise or object, perhaps a child's Lego.

Your Bible has a lot to say about light and we're going to jump to John 12. Since John speaks deeply on light and dark, we're going to spend a little time in this chapter. John 12:46 says, "I have come as a light to shine in this dark world so that all who put their trust in me will no longer remain in the dark."

There it is, the duality of light and dark. Pause for a moment. Have you ever been in a place where it's dark? Really dark?

Let's say you go camping in the woods. It doesn't matter where; you are now standing in the pitch black with just you and your dead flashlight. What if you are driving down an old country road and your headlights just suddenly stop working. How nervous are you right now?

Or maybe you got up late for a drink of water from the fridge. You head downstairs or around the bedroom corner to the kitchen. You're not going to turn lights on because you don't want to wake anybody up and you don't need the lights. Honestly, it's your house and you know where everything is. Do you remember that story about me scaring Hope in our laundry closet? Well, as sweet as my Hope is, she likes to get back at me for all my startles at night when it's dark.

I would get up in the middle of the night, I'd go get a drink of water from the fridge and I'd come back and head to the bathroom before getting back in bed. And sure enough, without fail, I'd walk in the bathroom, Hope would be standing around the corner, and she'd yell, "Ahhhh!" and my heart would stop. I'd head back to bed rattled and she would head back to bed giggling.

Even if you're in someplace familiar, when you are in the dark and there's that unexpected sound, your heart starts to race, and you start to try to hastily figure out what made the sound. In that moment, something changes. Your home goes from a place of peace that you know so well to one that is mysterious, and maybe even a little scary.

When you think about light and darkness, it's important to understand that light is so vital to our existence. Why? Let's look at scripture. When you read from Genesis, it's interesting to me that light is the very first thing God created. He started off in Genesis 1:3, "Let there be light." God creates light first and light overcame darkness by God's word. By His Spirit, light is still overcoming darkness. John begins his side of Christ's story with creation.

In the beginning the Word already existed.
The Word was with God,
and the Word was God.
He existed in the beginning with God.
God created everything through him,
and nothing was created except through him.
The Word gave life to everything that was created,
and his life brought light to everyone.
The light shines in the darkness, and the darkness
can never extinguish it. John 1:1-5

This is the apostle John's testimony as he writes about Jesus. He says that Jesus IS the very Word of God. Jesus is at the center of creation and He IS the light of the world. Look at verse 5. Like, really look at it. The light shines in the darkness, and the darkness can *never extinguish it.* Another translation says, *never comprehend it.* Another translation says, never overcome it.

Let's look at this a different way. I know we are talking about spiritual darkness, but we can gain so much from a good illustration. Imagine for a minute you're in a dark place. *You know, blind people have been figuring out how to navigate in the darkness for ages.* Yes, I know, what I want you to do is just picture the darkest place you can, one where you DON'T know where everything is. You try to call out for help. "I need light." Your best friend says, "I've got you, buddy," and then they hand you a hammer. A hammer is super helpful if that's what you need, but in this moment, a hammer cannot help you.

If you call out for help and somebody hands you a tuna fish sandwich, well, first of all, when you taste it and find out it's a tuna fish sandwich, the proper response is to throw it back at them. Then say, "Tuna fish is gross." Regardless, while you are

Nothing substitutes for light.

standing in the dark, nothing can substitute for light. Let me repeat that: **Nothing substitutes for light.** Not hammers, not sandwiches, not anything. Period. Nothing can be a substitute for light.

Jesus has come as light into the world. Receiving Jesus as God's light fulfills the purpose God has for us. Receiving the light of Jesus means having faith in God, that is, trusting God as the source of light, trusting the light of God's truth, trusting that God's light brightens the darkness of our days, and trusting that God's light gives us hope and rest. In Matthew 11:28 Jesus says that all who come to Him **shall find rest in Him**.

In 2008 Stormie Omartian wrote a book called *Just Enough Light For The Step I'm On,* based on Psalm 119:105: "Your word is a lamp to my feet and a light to my path." In her book she describes how we all want to know God's plans for our lives. But God, in His grace, mercy and wisdom, prevents us from seeing or knowing too much. We need only to let God—His light, His Word, His truth—enter into our hearts, and we find that God provides enough for us to withstand all that we face. We may want more, but we can only handle so much.

Your love, Lord, reaches to the heavens,
your faithfulness to the skies.
Your righteousness is like the highest mountains,
your justice like the great deep.
You, Lord, preserve both people and animals.

How priceless is your unfailing love, O God!
People take refuge in the shadow of your wings.
They feast on the abundance of your house;
you give them drink from your river of delights.
For with you is the fountain of life;
in your light we see light. Psalm 36:5-9

When we trust God, His Word, and His light, we begin to see that God is faithful and true, steadfast and unchanging, just as He says.

There are times when world events and personal tragedies seem to plunge us into darkness and we may feel that the light has been snuffed out; but the Bible affirms that whatever happens, God's light in Jesus light still shines, even today. We just need to take Him at His word.

Robert Fulghum wrote a book titled *All I Really Need to Know I Learned in Kindergarten.* Let me paraphrase for you what Fulgham shared as he was visiting an institute dedicated to reconciling Turks and Greeks on the island of Crete.

At the end of the visit, he asked a man named Alexandros Papanderos, a leader there, what the purpose of life was. After a while, Papanderos took from his wallet a small round mirror, no bigger than a quarter. He talked about his childhood during the war. About how one day, on the road he found a broken mirror. He told Fulghum about how he kept the largest piece. The very same piece that he pulled from his wallet. Papanderos became fascinated with it, noticing that it could reflect light into dark places where the sun would never shine. Now, as a man, he understood that the mirror and light were a metaphor for what we can do with our lives. Papanderos then described how we are each a fragment of a mirror whose whole design we do not yet know. We each have the power to reflect light. Moreover we can reflect truth, understanding, meaning, knowledge into the black places in the hearts of people. That the light has the power to provoke change.

In this same way, we each have the power to reflect whatever light we can so we can give light to those who are in darkness.

Do all things without grumbling or disputing, that you may be blameless and innocent, children of God without blemish in the midst of a crooked and twisted generation, among whom you shine as lights in the world, holding fast to the word of life, so that in the day of Christ I may be proud that I did not run in vain or labor in vain. Philippians 2:14-16 (ESV)

Shine - To give off or REFLECT light!

Jesus said, "Let your light shine before others" (Matthew 5:16a NIV).

When you cast HIS light, always point back to the light source. When Jesus said, "Let your light shine before others," that wasn't the whole sentence. He went on to give the reason why it's important to shine: "so that they may see your good deeds and glorify your Father in heaven." Never forget to share where your light is coming from!

The true light, which gives light to everyone, was coming into the world. John 1:9 (ESV)

He's the sun, and we're all His moons. He is the real light, while we are reflectors of His light, that's all.

For God, who said, "Let there be light in the darkness," has made this light shine in our hearts so we could know the glory of God that is seen in the face of Jesus Christ. 2 Corinthians 4:6

___

In other words, *God, who first ordered the light to shine in the darkness, has flooded our hearts with His light. We now can enlighten men, only because we can give them knowledge of the glory of God as we have seen it in the face of Jesus Christ.*

The beginning of verse 16 says, "Let your light shine." You don't have to crank it up. You don't have to light it yourself. You don't have to worry about getting it started or the batteries being dead; all you've got to do is *let it* shine!

Don't let it shine just among those you know who are also in the light. Let it shine before men, in the presence of those who would hate you, kill you, reject you, and deny you. Let it shine and let them see the beauty of your works. When you hide your testimony, you're not doing anything but preventing somebody from seeing the beauty of God Himself. When you don't testify, you're just withholding from someone that which they desperately need to see if they are ever to come to know God. Yes, being a light even to your enemies can be painful, but there can be purpose connected to your pain. You don't need a light in the middle of the day when there aren't any clouds in the sky! You need a light when things are dark!

Well, in God's light, we see light. If we'll tune our brains to see the blessing, the favor, the mercy, the goodness, the faithfulness, the strength, the power, and the grace of our God, then we begin to see it everywhere we look. It's why Philippians 4:8 says, "Finally, brothers, whatever is true, noble, lovely; of a good report, anything praiseworthy or virtuous, think on these things" (paraphrased).

Think on these things. Why? That is because if you begin to focus on the good things about God, you'll see it everywhere you look. Why? Because our God is faithful, strong, and true. He never fails. His goodness is on display all around us. Everywhere we look, all we must do is stay in His light. We're now able to see the light. If you're looking around you, and it just seems like everything is dark all the time, I would really encourage you to go back to Philippians 4:8. What are the things you're allowing yourself to think about? When we trust God, His Word, and His light, we begin to see that God is faithful and true, steadfast and unchanging, just like He promises.

STAND UP AND BE HEARD.

What does it mean to shine? The definition of *shine* is to give off or to reflect light. We must stand up and be heard. Jesus said, "Let your light shine before others." In Matthew 5:16, He explained that no one lights a lamp just to hide it under a basket. A lamp is meant to be placed on a stand and to give light to everything around it. Whether you're timid or outgoing, you're called to be a light to the people around you. And it's only possible if you're taking time to engage and cultivate relationships with the people around you.

> **Whether you're timid or outgoing, you're called to be a light to the people around you.**

For those of us who go to the gym, have you ever seen the "really big guy"? You know who I am talking about. He's always super, super intense. He's the guy in the gym who always has a scowl on his face, and he's built like he's been at the gym his whole life. This is not his first day here. As a matter of fact, he's done. He could go home now, but instead, he's at the gym and he's very focused. Honestly, for a guy like me, he's kind of intimidating.

Normally, when I go to the gym I am on a mission. I have my earbuds in, and I'm not here to talk or visit. I just want to **work out and get out**. I have other things I need to be doing. But this particular week, at the food drive, I accidentally brought my earbuds with me and put them in my friend Dan's truck. Therefore, I didn't have my earbuds, and trust me, that was by God's providence. What makes me think so? This big guy walks past me and immediately the Holy Spirit just quickens me to say hi. "Hey, man, how are you doing?"

I'm telling you he would've been less shocked if I'd just drop-kicked him on the spot. He stammered a little. "I'm sorry. What?" I repeated it. "Hey, man, how are you doing?" He stopped for a moment, as if to gather his thoughts. Almost to decide if he is going with the cliché answer of, *I'm good*, or if he is going to be honest. Finally, he answered, "I'm doing my best, man. I'm hanging in. I'm just trying to make it, okay." His honest response surprised me too.

So, I see this big, burly guy and he's kind of stomping. He's got his determined face on, and I interrupted his moment. What started as a small conversation at the gym led to coffee; and as I spend time with him, he starts to pour his heart out! When that happens, you have an opportunity to be light to someone unexpectedly. I realized, *He may look gruff or intimidating, he might have a scowl on his face when he is at the gym, but he's human just like me.*

I'm supposed to let my light shine. What does that mean? First and foremost, I must step out. But here's the cool part: God doesn't say, *Make your light shine.* He doesn't say, *Force your light to shine.* He says, **let your light shine**. The light is already there. You just need to let what is already inside of you shine! You have hope and joy in your life. Why? Because you have Jesus. You don't have to force it; you just let it show. One of the trainers at the gym where I work out is named Jeremy. Every time he sees me, even when I have a mask on, he says, "Man, Pastor Lafe, you just keep smiling. Your smile is contagious."

In the same way, there's going to be a smile on your face. There's going to be joy in your step. And when people see you, they're going to say, *"Hey, man, keep on smiling. Your smile's contagious."* Just as an FYI, my smile isn't something special. It's not that I've got the best smile in the world, and all other smiles suck. (Yes, I am a pastor, and I just used "suck" in a sentence.) It's not that my smile is better than yours. I'm just really used to letting it shine. It's something we can all do. We just let it shine. Stop trying to force it. Just let your light shine. And by the way, that is not dependent on being extroverted or introverted. It's not dependent on whether you're comfortable letting your light shine.

Here's the goodness of our God! You may be an introvert like one of my great friends, Seth. He is one of the most genuine, loving, and gracious people you're ever going to meet! But he's crazily introverted. You wouldn't catch him at the gym saying hi to everyone. I would never expect him to shine his light that way. That isn't how God made him. If you're an introvert, I'm not saying you must force yourself to be an extrovert. I'm not trying to say you should fake it. Just be genuine to who you are and brave enough to pursue God knowing in the fullness of who you are that He made you perfect just the way you are. You might be walking through some stuff and there might be some stuff that you should get rid of or let go of; but God made you who you are because He is going to send you across people's paths who need the introverted you to be just as you are. They won't need an extrovert like me. If you're an introvert, that's okay; let your light shine. If you're an extrovert, loud and over the top, be that. Just let your light shine. Stand up and be heard.

Let's look at Acts 16:16-30 for a minute.

One day as we were going down to the place of prayer, we met a slave girl who had a spirit that enabled her to tell the future. She earned a lot of money for her masters, by telling fortunes. She followed Paul and the rest of us, shouting, "These men are servants of the Most High God, and they have come to tell you how to be saved."

This went on day after day until Paul got so exasperated that he turned and said to the demon within her, "I command you in the name of Jesus Christ to come out of her." And instantly it left her.

Her masters' hopes of wealth were now shattered, so they grabbed Paul and Silas and dragged them before the authorities at the marketplace. "The whole city is in an uproar because of these Jews!" they shouted to the city officials. "They are teaching customs that are illegal for us Romans to practice."

A mob quickly formed against Paul and Silas, and the city officials ordered them stripped and beaten with wooden rods. They were severely beaten, and then they were thrown into prison. The jailer was ordered to make sure they didn't escape. So the jailer put them into the inner dungeon and clamped their feet in the stocks.

Around midnight Paul and Silas were praying and singing hymns to God, and the other prisoners were listening. Suddenly, there was a massive earthquake, and the prison was shaken to its foundations. All the doors immediately flew open, and the chains of every prisoner fell off! The jailer woke up to see the prison doors wide open. He assumed the prisoners had escaped, so he drew his sword to kill himself. But Paul shouted to him, "Stop! Don't kill your-self! We are all here!"

The jailer called for lights and ran to the dungeon and fell down trembling before Paul and Silas. Then he brought them out and asked, "Sirs, what must I do to be saved?" Acts 16:16-30

Paul and Silas praised at midnight and ALL the prisoners' chains fell off, not just theirs! When WE shine our light, OTHERS are set free!!! Paul and Silas could have been down and out about being put in prison again. Instead, their light set others free! Including the jailer! Are you someone who is constantly talking about the goodness of your God, or are you constant-ly complaining about your circumstance? Are they saying, "Something is different AND AMAZING about that guy," or are they saying, "Man, that guy's got issues!"?

Shining your light gives you the chance to show others that no matter what is happening in your life, you will lift your hands and praise God through the mess! You will praise God in the middle of any storm! When all is said and done, that's how you shine. Don't let the enemy dim your light with the troubles of this world. Instead, just LET the light of God inside of you shine.

PUT IT TO WORK

A city on a hill cannot be hidden.

Have there been times when you feel that life has snuffed out your light and left you in darkness?

Jesus has come as light into the world. The Bible affirms that whatever happens, the light of Jesus still shines. We just need to take Him at His word.

What can you intentionally do today to shine the light of who Jesus is in your circumstance?

The purpose of light is to shine. Can others see your faith and trust in God?

Often, the best witness you can give is NOT a well-crafted argument in favor of God. The BEST witness we can BE for the lost and hurting is demonstrating that God is real by your joy and peace, proving He is real by your love for others, and showing He is real by your confident Hope in the future.

_____

_____

_____

_____

_____

_____

_____

_____

_____

_____

_____

_____

_____

_____

_____

_____

_____

_____

_____

_____

_____

_____

11

ENOUGH PURPOSE

Purpose. There have been millions of books written on just this topic alone. While I am not going to spend an entire book on "purpose," I want to clarify the difference between a God-given purpose and chasing after the purposes of this world. As we go prayerfully into this chapter, I want to lay a foundation for a clear understanding of what happens when we know that our purpose is found in Christ, not in this world!

When God gives us a purpose and a calling, it isn't just an email from your boss giving you the to do list for today, and then leaving you to figure it out. God goes with you, and He goes before you, and He's always beside you! We don't ever walk through life alone. What's more, we can walk with boldness and confidence, because that's what He tells us to do. Let me show you what I mean:

After the death of Moses the servant of the Lord, the Lord said to Joshua, son of Nun, Moses' aide: "Now then, Moses my servant is dead. Now, you and all these people, get ready to cross the Jordan River into the land I am about to give to them—to the Israelites. I will give you every place where you set your foot, as I promised Moses. Your territory will extend from the desert to Lebanon, and from the great river, the Euphrates—all the Hittite country—to the Mediterranean Sea in the west. No one will be able to stand against you all the days of your life. As I was with Moses, so I will be with you; I will never leave you nor forsake you. Be strong and courageous, because you will lead these people to inherit the land I swore to their ancestors to give them.

"Be strong and very courageous. Be careful to obey all the law my servant Moses gave you; do not turn from it to the right or to the left, that you may be successful wherever you go. Keep this Book of the Law always on your lips; meditate on it day and night, so that you may be careful to do everything written in it. Then you will be prosperous and successful. Have I not commanded you? Be strong and courageous. Do not be afraid; do not be discouraged, for the Lord your God will be with you wherever you go." Joshua 1:1-9 (NIV)

As you and I begin a journey to understand God's purpose (not the world's) we need to begin with an understanding that we can do so with authority, power, and strength. There is a danger that comes with not knowing or understanding your purpose or calling. Let me give you the most basic example. See, I'm a car guy, and when I say *I'm a car guy,* I don't mean that I'm a hot rod guy, or motorsport guy. I mean I just really like cars and knowing all the different things about them. If I see a car on the road and don't recognize the make and model, it becomes a mystery that I need to solve. I'll speed up or slow down to try to see the logo on the car, and who made it. Then when I get home, I look it up to find out more about it.

So, several years ago, Toyota came out with the Avalon. Now, to give you some context, Toyota owns Lexus. If you buy a nice enough Toyota, they include a really fancy Lexus badge instead of the Toyota one. The year I saw the Avalon, it was the highest-level Toyota you could buy without it being a Lexus. It had all the bells and whistles. The fanciest of the fancy Toyotas you could get. Once I had researched everything, I started to keep an eye out for it. Well, I'm driving through McKinney, Texas, and spot one—a brand-new Toyota Avalon pulls in front of me. This thing looked like it had just rolled off the showroom floor.

Then something caught my attention. This brand-new Avalon already had a bumper sticker on it. You must be really passionate about something to put a sticker on a brand-new car. It only had one sticker . . . just one. This guy must really care about this. What do you think this guy (with this really nice, fancy, expensive, not to mention brand-new car) wants to pro-claim to the world? What's the one thing on his mind that he wants you to know most about him? You couldn't guess in a million years.

The bumper sticker said, "I'm a smoker and I vote."

That's the ONE THING you want to say to the world?!? That's it???

I want to make sure you know this one thing about me: It's super important to me that you know, I'm a smoker and I vote. Just a little heads-up.

What is the point of this story? When we do not understand our purpose and our calling, we can begin to identify ourselves in unhealthy ways. Our personal "bent" (interests, desires, passions) becomes our identity. That is so dangerous. The truth of the matter is, when we don't understand our destiny, our purpose and calling, we begin to identify solely by what we think it is that makes us unique. *What is it about me that's different? What is it about me that sets me apart?* You plant your flag in an identity that doesn't belong to you. We will even do that with a vice. Nobody grows up and says, "I can't wait to start smoking." Yet, we can be so unsure of what we are really supposed to be living for that we will live for whatever's in front of us. That leads us to believe, *"This is my thing. I'm a smoker and I vote."* If we would just pause long enough to understand that when we shrink our world down to the size of our personal issues, we've missed out on so much of life. Why? God's purpose and plan for us is so much bigger than that. If we don't understand we're made for a purpose, then the bumps and bruises of life begin to reduce our personal value, one bump and bruise at a time. Have you ever lost your job? Fought a debilitating illness? It is far too easy for us to label ourselves with the pain and suffering in this world.

How have you labeled yourself? When we don't understand our purpose, it can be easy to grasp onto whatever adds "value" to our lives. Labels are treacherous.

How can we plant our flag where God wants us to, if we don't understand our purpose and identity?

When you don't understand your identity, you begin to tie your identity to one of two things: what has happened to you or what you have achieved. Let's start with the danger of achievements. Let's say you are really successful at your job, and you earn promotion after promotion and raise after raise. *"I'm a success! I'm valuable! This is who I am!"* But what about when a pay cut comes? Or a job loss? If you measure your worth by your achievements and then face a pay cut, you begin to believe that you aren't just worth less, but over time you'll begin to believe that you are *worthless*. This happens because we have put our identity, our destiny, and our purpose within the confines of a box that is of this world. When we don't understand what our purpose is, we'll begin to identify with all the wrong things. That identity may work for a while, but eventually there will be an attack against our worth.

Maybe you don't struggle with your identity in your achievements; maybe you struggle with an identity that is shaped out of what's happened to you. Your identity can be built on hurts, rejections, and pains of the past. If that's the case, then over time our identity becomes that of "victim."

As we struggle with that, and as the bumps and bruises continue to come, little by little we see ourselves as worth less and less. Nothing will keep you bound to a single moment in time like unforgiveness and bitterness. God wants so much more for you than that! If that is stirring in your heart at all, please go back and read chapter 7 one more time.

> **It is critical that you understand you have a purpose and a calling.**

It is critical that you—yes, I'm talking to you, the unique and deeply loved person reading this book—it is critical you understand that you have a purpose and a calling. Not a single one of us is without one. If you don't know what it is yet, that's okay. Just hang on because we are going to get there.

Before we go any further, understand that not knowing your purpose places you in a dangerous season. *Why?* Because if you don't know what your purpose or calling is, the world is ready to offer suggestions. The world has a thousand different ways to tell you what your purpose and your calling is. Trust me, the world has no clue. God made you for a purpose; what the world offers is a cheap counterfeit.

YOU WERE MADE FOR A PURPOSE!

How do I know this?

"Before I formed you in the womb I knew you, before you were born, I set you apart. I appointed you as a prophet to the nations." "Alas, Sovereign Lord," I said, "I do not know how to speak; I am too young." But the Lord said to me, "Do not say, 'I am too young.' You must go to everyone I send you to and say whatever I command you. Do not be afraid of them, for I am with you and will rescue you," declares the Lord.

Then the Lord reached out his hand and touched my mouth and said to me, "I have put my words in your mouth. See, today I appoint you over nations and kingdoms to uproot and tear down, to destroy and overthrow, to build and to plant." Jeremiah 1:5-10 (NIV)

You may not be called as a prophet to the nations, but make no mistake, the same God that foreknew Jeremiah and the purpose he was created for knew the same about you before you were ever born. AND . . . while you may not be called to prophesy to nations, you have the same purpose to speak God's Word and advance His kingdom. You were made to declare God's goodness, His mercy, His kindness, His love, and His graciousness. You were made to take His light into dark places.

The Spirit of the Sovereign Lord is on me, because the Lord has anointed me to proclaim good news to the poor. He has sent me to bind up the brokenhearted, to proclaim freedom for the captives, to release from darkness the prisoners, to proclaim the year of the Lord's favor and the day of vengeance of our God, to comfort all who mourn, and provide for those who grieve in Zion—to bestow on them a crown of beauty instead of ashes, the oil of joy instead of mourning, and a garment of praise instead of a spirit of despair. They will be called oaks of righteousness, a planting of the Lord for the display of his splendor. Isaiah 61:1-3

Jesus quotes this same passage as a fulfillment of prophecy in Luke 4:18. This is your purpose! This is our calling!

But don't we have a purpose and a calling that is specific to us individually? ABSOLUTELY! But your purpose and your calling are never outside of the scope found in Luke 4:18. Let me break this down. You WEREN'T called to be a world-famous singer, or actor, or athlete, or millionaire. THAT is not your purpose! However, if you'll be faithful to declare God's love, His mercy, and His goodness. If you'll declare the love of Jesus, then the avenue God uses to position us may very well be your music, your athletic ability, or your business.

So how can I know what God's specific purpose is for me?

Can I please take some pressure off you? I've heard "God's will" and "God's purpose" referred to as if it is some unknowable mystery that we have to somehow solve, as if we have to find a pebble on some far distant seashore. No wonder we become so stressed about God's will for us. It isn't nearly so difficult. It's taking the next step in front of you to follow Jesus. Whatever that step is! Be faithful in this moment . . . and you are on your way.

I cannot tell you what your unique purpose is, but I can tell you how to discover it: SERVE! Serve wherever you are, whatever way you can, serve with a purpose of reaching people for God's kingdom. If you do that, your purpose will find you! I'm a living example that it's true!

Now, this is not "Serve God until your next promotion presents itself," because that keeps YOU as the central focus of your life. If instead you choose to serve wherever you are, whatever the specific need is at that moment, serve for the Lord, not for self-fulfillment, then you will absolutely find joy and fulfillment in serving. Be careful not to let your heart lead you to serve for selfish reasons.

Our congregation (at the time of this writing) meets in a local school for our services. That means every week we unload all of our equipment and supplies off of a truck. Then someone must set up the chairs, lights, sound system, and children's ministry equipment.

Listen, I don't think anybody's gift is to unload a truck, but it's got to be done, right? Somebody's got to do it. If somebody doesn't unload the truck, set the chairs in place, put the lights in place, and put the cameras in place, we can all miss out on what God wants to do. He wants to proclaim His goodness and His love for His people. If we are not willing to do whatever it takes to serve Him, then

If we are not willing to do whatever it takes to serve Him, then we'll never find what our purpose is.

we'll never find what our purpose is. Why? As it says in James 2:26, *"Faith without works is dead"* (KJV). God is saying to us first and foremost, "Get up and get involved."

In 1990 Henry Blackaby wrote a book called *Experiencing God* which specifically talks about mature Christians not doing what is common. Throughout my years in ministry, I have heard these words countless times: *I need God to come to me. I need God to come to me where I'm at right now. I need God to come invade my circumstance.* I need God to *be here.* The tricky part about this is it can derail us and make God into our genie instead of our Lord and King. If we're always asking God to come to where we are and serve our needs right now, our value is still bound up in the world.

Perhaps, instead we should say, "God, I'll go wherever you send me." In the book *Experiencing God,* by Henry and Richard Blackaby, they explain that mature Christians aren't waiting to experience God or demanding that God come to where they are time after time to rescue them. Instead, they are instead looking for where God is moving and then they go get involved in His work. If you want God to use you, go where He is moving. Don't demand God continue over and over to come and rescue you. Don't continue to ask God to raise you up, and do something amazing through you if you aren't willing to be an active part of what He is already doing.

Serving where you are on whatever level you can is an AMAZING tool to discover God's plans and purpose for you. But . . . there's a danger here too.

A true servant's heart serves out of love and gratitude, not selfish ambition. If we're not careful, we can start to seek positions and recognition rather than the heart of God.

James Hutchins, who pastors New Life Community Church in Frisco, Texas, is my mentor and a friend of mine. He lives not too far from me and every time we get together, I learn so much. One particular time we were talking about a situation that had come up and he said, "Lafe, you have to be careful. Anybody who introduces themself with their title first is a red flag. Run away." This is especially important when we're talking about kingdom stuff.

Long before I was ever ordained as a pastor I had been told I had a pastor's heart. My pastor at the time even spoke over me the day I was ordained, and said, "Lafe, you have already been a pastor. You have a pastor's heart. Now we're just going to make it official." I didn't start with a pastor's heart. I mean I always cared about people and always had a desire to help. I learned to have a pastor's heart as I served in different areas of the church. God developed that heart in me as I began serving. Over time my heart shifted. I moved from volunteering in the church (task oriented) to serving people in church. How? I prayed a dangerous prayer. *"God, help me see people the way you see them."* I didn't start serving in church as a pathway to someday having the title of "pastor." I didn't even know that was possible. I saw God moving in the hearts of people, I saw lives impacted, I saw hope restored. Like Henry Blackaby said, I saw God moving and knew I had to be a part of it.

Serve God where you are and let Him define you. The alternative is accepting the labels that the world will try to place on you. When we allow the world to label us, we become more and more polarized. While there are a lot of great things about social media and staying connected to friends and loved ones with instant updates, there's an insidious threat just under the surface. *Meta-filters* is the term I've heard used. It sounds helpful and sweet. There's an algorithm that monitors the things you like or "heart," the news articles you click on and read, as well as who your friends are. The idea is to highlight or show you more of the things you like when you open social media; but the danger is that you only ever see things you already agree with. The algorithm labels you as liberal or conservative, pro this and anti that, and it continues to feed you more and more of the things that it identifies with you. The danger is that the more we consume, the more we're exposed to, the more we see that affirms the way we see the world, the LESS we are able to see anyone else's point of view. Maybe that doesn't sound so bad, but it's happening on the other side of the ideological spectrum as well. We are more and more biased because we can truly believe that everyone we see agrees with our point of view and that anyone who DOESN'T agree must be either evil or stupid.

I may step on some toes in this next part, but I know that if it stings, it is usually because I hit an open nerve we need to address. There is this notion that if someone doesn't believe the same way as you that they must be evil or stupid. This causes each of us to become more and more dogmatic. Maybe you tell others your purpose is to serve God, yet all your social media posts are some combination of mask or no mask, Black Lives Matter or All Lives Matter, defund the police or back the blue, and I could go on and on with this, but this separation of isolated opinions creates the division we so desperately need to rebuke. *Lemme tell you about me. I'm a smoker and I vote... if you don't see things the way I do then you must hate me. I in turn will choose to hate you.*

We talk about purpose and about serving God but look at what's being displayed in our lives. Have you turned your life over to serving God's kingdom? Is your life about God or is your life about your issues? We can become lost to our purpose in a seemingly subtle way. God has given you a purpose to love Him and love people. To reach people with the good news that God loves them. How can you ever achieve your purpose if you're so convinced that everybody who doesn't agree with you is either evil or stupid and not worth your time? You will lose any desire or drive to go reach them and tell them about a God who loves them, who wants to restore them, heal them, and raise them up.

Jonah hated the Ninevites so much that he felt they didn't deserve God's mercy, so he tried to avoid God's purpose for him. When God took him to Nineveh anyway, Jonah prayed that they wouldn't receive the good news he'd just preached. That's CRAZY! But that could be us. If we make our lives about our issues, it WILL be us. I can assure you that your purpose has nothing to do with your issues.

Now, before you throw this book across the room, I'm not saying you can't have a purpose and still have a viewpoint on "mask or no mask," but there is nothing that should define you more than how you are a child of God, created in His image for one reason: to make His name famous in the earth, to spread His kingdom, to advance His Word. To show others they can be healed, restored, and lifted up. To prove that they don't have to be in bondage. You don't have to be a prisoner. You can get up.

Luke 4:18 says, *"The spirit of the Lord is upon me, for he has anointed me to bring good news to the poor."*

This is your purpose. This is your calling. Anything else that doesn't align with Luke 4:18 means you're missing it already. Our issues should never supersede our calling and our purpose. Write down that scripture. Bury it in your heart, and when in doubt always come back to Luke. We should stop making our lives about our issues. *I'm a smoker and I vote.* Don't make it about your political leanings. Again, I'm not saying you can't have a belief system. I'm not saying you can't know who you're going to vote for in November. The takeaway here is that when you rail on people about your beliefs, you need to realize that it isn't going to change how they see things. During the pandemic it was so easy to see the division with the "mask or no mask" argument. When you shadow people in Walmart for not wearing a mask, or you tell people who are wearing a mask that they're sheep, how is that building the kingdom of God?

You're a sheep for wearing a mask!

You are evil and stupid for NOT wearing a mask!

You know what's really hard? Calling someone stupid, evil, or a sheep, and then turning around to tell them that God loves them.

"You're an idiot! Oh, by the way, do you want to come to church with me on Sunday?"

REFUSING TO BE REDEFINED

When you find your purpose, remember that there will likely be resistance. The culture surrounding us will try to redefine you and then push and bully you into living by their definition of you.

During the third year of King Jehoiakim's reign in Judah, King Nebuchadnezzar of Babylon came to Jerusalem and be-sieged it. The Lord gave him victory over King Jehoiakim of Judah and permitted him to take some of the sacred objects from the Temple of God. So Nebuchadnezzar took them back to the land of Babylonia and placed them in the trea-sure-house of his god. Then the king ordered Ashpenaz, his chief of staff, to bring to the palace some of the young men of Judah's royal family and other noble families, who had been brought to Babylon as captives. "Select only strong, healthy, and good-looking young men," he said. "Make sure they are well versed in every branch of learning, are gifted with knowledge and good judgment, and are suited to serve in the royal palace. Train these young men in the language and literature of Babylon." The king assigned them a daily ration of food and wine from his own kitchens. They were to be trained for three years, and then they would enter the roy-al service. Daniel, Hananiah, Mishael, and Azariah were four of the young men chosen, all from the tribe of Judah. The chief of staff renamed them with these Babylonian names:

Daniel was called Belteshazzar. Hananiah was called Shadrach. Mishael was called Meshach. Azariah was called Abednego. Daniel 1:1-7

In modern American culture, we pick names because we like the way they sound or the way they go together. Maybe we pick our kids' names because we like alliteration.

Names were a very big deal at the time of Daniel. Names held meaning. Names were also a sign of ownership. The re-naming of the young men here was more than just an "adapt to our culture" thing. They gave them new names to mark a "new revelation" that they might forsake their former faith and country. The renaming was an attack against their purpose! The Babylonians tried to change and to co-opt their purpose.

- Daniel in Hebrew meant "God is my judge." Belteshazzar meant "Fair one, protect the king." Another translation says, "Preserve thou (O Bel) his life" or "prince of Bel" (Bel was a chief deity of Babylon and a god of beauty).

- Hananiah in Hebrew meant "Yahweh has been gracious." Shadrach meant "Inspired or illumined by the sun god."

- Mishael in Hebrew meant "Who is what God is?" (or "Who is like our God?"). Meshach meant, "I am despised, contempt-ible, and humiliated"; another translation kept "mi" or "who is like" but dropped El which was a Hebrew name for God and substituted "Shach" which was short for Sheshach, the Chaldean goddess of the earth.

- Azariah in Hebrew meant "Yahweh has helped" or "the one whom God helps." Abednego meant "servant of Nebo" or "Servant of the Shining Fire."

So, what happened in the renaming of these four servants of God is that the Babylonians substituted names that dedicated them to the service of the four principal gods of the Chaldeans or Babylonians. Bel was their chief god, then their sun god, the earth god, and the fire god. If we aren't careful, our culture, unhealthy people in your life, our own fears and insecurities will try to "rename" us, to steal our identity and make it something much less, and to rob us of our purpose.

You are no accident, no matter what anyone says.

When culture shifts, you GOTTA know who you are!!

Let me say this again. If we're not careful, our culture, or the unhealthy people in our lives, our own fears and insecurities will try to rename us and steal our identity. To change it and make it something else, something that robs us of our purpose.

The most important thing that you allow yourself to be identified as **is who God says you are.**

You are no accident, no matter what anyone says. I repeat this for good measure because I want you to imbed this into your spirit: **You are no accident.** You were custom designed and built by God for a divine purpose. You were chosen for this moment in history and in this place for a purpose: to make an impact for His kingdom.

PUT IT TO WORK

If you ask someone what their purpose in life is, often times they will begin to look concerned, and if they're honest they might even reply, "I'm not really sure." Somehow, we've made the question of purpose into an intimidating mystery, DOUBLY so when you ask, "what is GOD's purpose for your life?"

Do you know what your purpose is? Is it about your success in business, in family, or even in ministry? If so, it might be time to take another look.

Thankfully, when God gives you a purpose and a calling, He doesn't leave you to figure it out alone. God goes with you, and He goes before you, and He's always beside you!

What's one thing you can do to step out in faith today? Finding God's purpose isn't about solving a mystery; it's about following God's lead and taking the next step.

12

ENOUGH POWER

Discovering your purpose is vital, but without power to walk it out, our purpose remains unfulfilled! Purpose is important; it's the rudder that steers your ship, but how can we truly live in the purpose that God has for us if we don't understand the very power that He has placed within each of us? Without power, the rudder can't direct your path. I think it's safe to say that if you are reading this book then you believe in God, you believe that He is good, and you believe that He is not short on power. Doubt comes in when we fail to believe and understand the part where God says He's going to put that kind of power in us. We don't doubt for a second that God can and does do miracles; we just doubt that He would ever do miracles . . . through US.

So where in scripture does it say God is going to put THAT kind of power in us?

I pray that out of his glorious riches he may strengthen you with power through his Spirit in your inner being, so that Christ may dwell in your hearts through faith. And I pray that you, being rooted and established in love, may have power, together with all the Lord's holy people, to grasp how wide and long and high and deep is the love of Christ, and to know this love that surpasses knowledge—that you may be filled to the measure of all the fullness of God. Now to him who is able to do immeasurably more than all we ask or imagine, according to his power that is at work within us, to him be glory in the church and in Christ Jesus throughout all generations, for ever and ever! Amen. Ephesians 3:16-21 (NIV)

*"Don't you believe that I am in the Father, and that the Father is in me? The words I say to you I do not speak on my own authority. Rather, it is the Father, living in me, who is doing His work. Believe me when I say that I am in the Father and the Father is in me; or at least believe on the evidence of the works themselves. Very truly I tell you, whoever believes in me will do the works I have been doing, and **they will do even greater things than these,** because I am going to the Father" (emphasis mine). John 14:10-12 (NIV)*

Did you catch that? He said we would do GREATER things! This is Jesus speaking, who raised the dead back to life. This is Jesus who healed the lepers, who raised up the crippled and lame to walk again. This is Jesus who restored sight to blind eyes. This is Jesus who multiplied five loaves and two fish to feed more than 5,000 people. This is Jesus. This passage in John 14 is Jesus' response to Phillip's request in John 14:8 when he said, "Lord, show us the Father and that will be enough for us." Jesus is surprised by Philip's request and asks, "Don't you know me, Philip?" He explains that He and His Father are one. The Father's in the Son, and the Son's in the Father. Yes, God's got power. That means that Jesus has that same power. Here's the part that's hard to even contemplate . . . Jesus said we'd do even greater things than the miracles we see Him doing (John 14:12)!

If you don't mind, can I redirect our thought process for a minute? I've never walked on water, I've never healed lepers, and I haven't raised one single person from the dead. I have prayed for the sick and seen them recover right in front of my eyes. You're too late to tell me that God doesn't still heal today! But overall, it doesn't SEEM like I'm doing anything all that amazing. Yet I've shared the gospel with someone who believed, made a new decision, and then shared the gospel with others. I have worked to feed the hungry and seen the very people I helped in one season be the ones to help others in the next season. I've been on evangelistic crusade teams around the world and seen multitudes respond.

When Jesus said that if we had faith as small as a mustard seed, we could move mountains, He didn't intend for His people to walk around trying to rearrange His creation just to test their faith. He meant that you and I, empowered by HIS authority and strength, could look at what seems impossible and make that mountain move! Jesus fed thousands; working together we can feed tens of thousands. Jesus preached to thousands; together we can bring the gospel to hundreds of thousands all over the world. Don't get hung up on your inability to walk on water. We should focus on the God-sized dream He's put in your heart! Do something about the broken and hurting people God has put in your path! Don't doubt for one second that the same miracle-working power that was in Jesus is in you!

A quote I love from A.W. Tozier says, *"God is looking for people through whom he can do the impossible. What a pity that we plan only the things we can do by ourselves."*

Don't get hung up on your inability to walk on water.

What prevents us from walking in the power that God intended for us? What blocks us from walking in the power that God says is already in us? Why aren't we able to confidently step out and walk in power when Jesus says we'll do even greater works?

We doubt that we have that kind of power in Christ because so often we know our own failings. We are consumed by our own guilt and shame. We doubt that God would put that kind of power into a flawed vessel like us. There's another power that we need to consider. The power of transformation. God is working out our own transformation with every step. It isn't about behavior modification. It's not about behaving like a good little Christian. It most definitely isn't about keeping the rules just right.

Make sure:

• Your hair isn't too long.

• You don't have too many tattoos.

• If you DO have tattoos make sure to keep them covered.

"I need to be a good little Christian now because I'm supposed to be transformed into the image of God." You can't transform yourself! That takes the power of the Holy Spirit working in us! It's not about following rules; it's about following Jesus! Christ came to set us free and yet we get hung up on behavior modification.

Let me paint you a picture. D.L. Moody was speaking to a large group of people, and he held up a glass and he said, "Somebody tell me how to get all the air out of this glass." Before you read on any further, tell me what YOU would do to get the air out.

The first man stood up in response and said, "Attach a vacuum and suck the air out."

D.L. Moody replied, "Well, that would create a vacuum in the glass and therefore shatter the glass. That's not going to be the best solution. We don't want to destroy the glass. What else?" Several more answers came about and none of them presented a good way to remove the air from the glass. After a while, without saying a word, D.L. Moody just picked up a pitcher of water, and poured water into the glass. He held up the glass and said, "It's done. All the air is out." He went on to explain that our faith doesn't work like some kind of vacuum pump sucking one sin or another out at a time during our walking with Jesus. Instead, our transformation is a product of our pouring more and more of who He is into us. Adding more and more of His Spirit into us so that there's no more room for those things that can hold us back.

So how *do we access the power that God has already given us?*

Well, for that we need to let go of all that we are and bring it to God. And I do mean all of it. Let's start with a few verses from Deuteronomy.

"Then build an altar there to the Lord your God, using natural, uncut stones. You must not shape the stones with an iron tool. Build the altar of uncut stones and use it to offer burnt offerings to the Lord your God. Also sacrifice peace offerings

on it and celebrate by feasting there before the Lord your God. Deuteronomy 27:5-7

God wanted unrefined, uncut, unperfected stones. Why? Why would God want uncut, unperfected stones?

One significant aspect of an "uncut" stone is that it is complete. If we remove or leave any part of the stone out it becomes a cut stone and not the kind of stone God is asking for.

"I like everything about this stone except this part. I'm sure that God doesn't want THIS part, so I'll cut it off and give Him everything else."

The moment you try to give Him some part of you but not ALL of you, you aren't presenting yourself as a whole offering. If we won't bring our whole lives to God like an unrefined stone, how can we expect to walk in the complete purpose He has for us?

Why don't we walk with the kind of power that Jesus said we're supposed to have?

It starts with doubt. We doubt ourselves because we are so covered up with guilt, shame, and insecurity that we doubt God would want to do anything with us. God says, "Listen, what you need is more of me. I'll deal with all your sin, guilt, and shame along the way. Nothing else will satisfy you. Not more of this world. Not more stuff, only more of me."

2 Peter 1:3-4 says,

"By his divine power, God has given us everything we need for living a godly life. We have received all this by coming to know him, the one who called us to himself by means of his marvelous glory and excellence. And because of his glory and excellence, he has given us great and precious promises. These are the promises that enable you to share in His

divine nature and escape the world's corruption caused by human desires."

When we get into self-doubt, guilt, or shame, we lose sight of how God sees us, His beloved child that He is restoring and transforming into His own image (2 Corinthians 3:18). What we need is more of Jesus. When we truly understand who He is and who we are in Him, we walk in power and authority.

What's another reason we don't walk in the kind of power that Jesus says we're supposed to walk in? It's hesitancy. We don't walk in the kind of power that we're supposed to walk in as a believer in Christ because of our own hesitancy. What does that look like? *"I wish God would just show me what I'm supposed to do,"* or *"I wish God would just tell me what to do next."*

But that's not the picture we get in the Bible. If anybody had direct access to God, it's the apostle Paul, right? Paul started more churches, did more mission trips, and raised up more pastors than anyone in the history of the early church. Doctrine that we still walk in today was established by Paul centuries ago. This is Paul who wrote a third of the New Testament. If anybody's got a direct line to God and knows what God wants them to do next, it's Paul, right?

We ask God to guide our steps, but then we step with hesitancy. What happens when we ask God to guide our steps, but then we don't step? Maybe Paul has some answers. Surely, he would ask God where to go and what he should be doing. As a matter of fact, it's interesting because Paul writes things like, "We thought it best to stay in Athens." He didn't say, *"God told me to stay in Athens."* He said, "We thought it best to stay in Athens. Another time, he said, "I had planned to come to you, but I was restrained." So, he's making plans for what to do next.

In all that he wrote to us, he's doing what he says he believes is best in the moment.

All right, so you are saying we're supposed to ask God to guide our steps, but then we're supposed to step out, is that right? Isn't it a good, godly, wise spiritual thing to wait until God tells me what to do?

You can't steer a parked car.

Doesn't that sound sweet, just waiting on God to lay out the perfect path? The problem is that you can't steer a parked car, right? "You can't steer a parked car." I've said that phrase a lot. I don't know where I first heard that phrase and there's no clear author to credit if you search it, but I've used it so many times that I just may claim it. Now, this isn't just a cliché sentence. I have personal experience with this because I taught our firstborn baby girl to drive. The day we decided to try it we were at my uncle's house. My uncle and aunt's house is in central Texas and I mean MILES away from anyplace in particular; they're out in the middle of nowhere. They have hundreds of acres. Have you ever had directions from a friend include the words, "Turn off the paved road"? Then you understand just the kind of nowhere where we were.

Let me preface this story by telling you that today my daughter is an excellent (albeit very cautious) driver!

So, Callie and I headed out to the truck. At the last second, I told her to hop in the driver's seat. She immediately turns white as a sheet. She'd been wanting to learn to drive, but now the moment was here.

"You want me to what?"

"It's okay, Sweet Girl. I got you. And look around. What are you going to hit? We're good." So, she got in the driver's seat, and I got in the passenger's seat.

"Okay, go ahead and put it in drive." (Sometimes we forget there are things we take for granted that others would know.)

"How do I do that?"

"Okay, here's what you're going to do: You're going to push on the brake pedal, that's the pedal on the left. Just put your shoe on it and mash it down, then take the shifter and move it down till you get to the D for drive." (She put it in drive.)

"Okay, go ahead and give it some gas." (I should have been more specific.)

"Take your foot off the brake first and THEN give it a little gas."

(She took her foot off the brake and the car began to eek forward.)

"Okay, give it some gas."

"Nope, we're going fast enough." (We were going MAYBE two miles an hour.)

Now this is a really long driveway and at the end of the driveway, it comes to a T. You can go left, or you can go right, but you can't go straight because straight puts you in a ditch.

After the long commute to the end of the driveway I said, "Let's go ahead and turn right."

You would think I just warned her that Sasquatch was right in front of us! She stomped on the brake and the car jerked to a full stop (at least we weren't going fast). Then she cranked the wheel as hard as she could to the right.

"Okay, that's one approach. Go ahead and give us some gas."

The next challenge was that every time she touched the gas pedal the truck now moved in a new direction. This was unnerving to a first-time driver, so she smashed the brake pedal. Let's just say it took a while to complete that turn.

Here's what I know for sure, because I have experience with this: You cannot steer a parked car. You can whip the wheel left or right, but you have not changed the car's destination. Changing your destination requires motion.

In Joshua 1, God tells him, "I'll be with you everywhere you go." In other words, "Wherever your foot steps, I'll give you that ground." What if Joshua had stood still? I can just imagine God looking at Joshua as he stood there, still as the grave.

"Listen, I want to give you whatever ground you step out onto, but you must step forward. You're going to have to take a step." Picture for a moment a mom or dad who's teaching their child to ride a bike. What do they do? They put the child on the bike, and they run along behind the bike keeping it upright, preventing the child from falling to the left or to the right. If the child does fall over, their mom or dad is going to be there to pick him back up. But it's up to the child to pedal and to steer.

Think about it this way. God will run alongside you as you learn to take more and more steps forward. Even knowing God is there, we think about walking out our faith and standing for something, and we just get scared. Why? As a child, you're thinking, *What if I run into a mailbox or what if I run into a parked car or worse, a moving car?* The good news is God's going to help steer you away from those things. How? Because He knows where all the mailboxes are. He's going to guide your steps. But for all His faithfulness, for all His provision, and for all His protection, you still have to pedal, and you still have to steer.

One more time: Why don't we operate in the kind of power and authority that God said we could have? If we have all His authority and the same power that raised Christ from the dead lives in us, why is it so hard to walk in that power?

Because we are so prone to hesitate. Think about our food ministry program. It started when we recognized a need in our community during the pandemic lockdown. Our local schools had food pantries for kids who were economically at risk. The shutdown meant a lot of families who were dependent on the next paycheck for groceries couldn't work. The school food pantries were empty before you could bat an eye. There was a need, and our church could do something about it. We didn't need to go fast and pray to find out if God would want us to act. We decided to act in faith because God put us in our community for such a time as this. It was faith because our church didn't have endless resources. In fact, it could have killed our church and burned up all the church's finances. Our church began providing food to the food pantries and because we took that step, we were invited to help distribute food. Because we took THAT step, God opened a door for us to do a mobile food bank once a month in the parking lot of the local high school. Because we took THAT step, a door opened for us to lease a little 3,000-square-foot building that needed a lot of work, but we turned it into a permanent food bank in our city where we now do food ministry three times a week.

God met us at every step, and not only did it not kill the church, but God kept blessing us with more and more resources to pour into the community. The pandemic could have killed our little start-up church, but instead our church exploded into a thriving family of believers who aren't content to just get together once a week. We understand that we've been called to make a difference right here where God planted us!

But what if we had never taken a step?

Then 250-plus families wouldn't have gotten the resources they needed in just ONE of our mobile food banks. How many more families have we cared for in the two and a half years since then? I have no idea, but we are so glad we didn't just stand by and wait to step.

"But God, I don't want to move until you tell me what to do." You are in danger of missing out on so much that God wants to do in you and through you.

We want God to tell us, *Go here,* or *Do this,* or *Say that.*

Can I say something that's going to sound "un-Christian"? I don't want to wait until God tells me what to do, what to say, where to go. To be clear, I <u>absolutely</u> want to wait on God based on the understanding that the Old Testament authors meant it!

For example, in Psalm 27:14 King David wrote, "Wait for the Lord; be strong, and in your heart take courage; wait for the Lord." That was right after he wrote, "Teach me your way, O Lord, and lead me on a level path" (v. 11 ESV).

Oftentimes, we mistakenly say "wait" as if it meant inaction. The word in Hebrew that's been translated as *wait* is קָוָה. It's pronounced "Kah-VAY."

Yes, one of the translations is "wait," but not in the sense of stillness. It also means to stretch, it means tension as in a rope; in fact one of the other definitions is a "measuring rope." In that sense, we are supposed to stay connected to the heart of God, to be stretched, to let Him lead us and guide our steps. Our God is on the move. Staying connected to Him, waiting on Him is like dancing in His rhythm. We are moving with Him as He is teaching us His ways and leading us in His paths. What an odd thing it is that when the path He's leading us on has challenges, our response is to stop and say we're waiting on God. He wants us to move with Him, move LIKE Him, and IN Him, to be a vessel He can use in an answer to someone's prayers.

Yes, there are times when the wisest thing we can do is to stop striving in our own strength and reconnect with His, but most often this happens when we've become disconnected. If

> **Our God is on the move.**

we stay connected, then we are on the move, following in the paths of our God.

If God must tell you step by step where to go, what to do, or what to say, you aren't walking in the kind of RELATIONSHIP He wants with you. You've been reduced to an unplugged robot. Besides, let's be real, if we knew where God ultimately wanted us to go with no preparation, we would absolutely say, "But I don't want to go there, God. That isn't what I meant by telling me where to go. I want you to tell me where *I* want to go."

He wants to walk beside you as you walk in His power because you're His beloved son or daughter. He loves you that much, and believe it or not, He trusts you that much. Think about the prodigal son. The prodigal son blows it as bad as anybody can blow it. Now all he can hope is that maybe his father will allow him to be a servant when he gets home. Instead, when he comes walking down the road that leads home and his father sees him, alive and well, his father comes running to him at the end of the road. What happens next? His father puts a robe on his shoulders (his covering, restored status as a son), and then he puts the ring (signifying the father's authority) on his son's finger.

The son who had blown it as badly as anyone, has access to all his father's authority and power? Yes, but more than that, the father says, "Here are some sandals, so you have the authority to walk where I walk and to walk WITH me. To top it all off, I'm going to throw you a feast just because I love you."

God created you in His image to bear His image in the world.

I want you to truly hear this. Deep in your heart. See, God has revealed His heart to you in His Word and through His Son. It is our joy, our privilege, to walk in relationship and partnership with our heavenly Father, and to be given the authority to go where He says to go; but He doesn't have to prescribe it specifically. When God told Joshua, "I'll give you whatever ground you walk on", He didn't say "take three steps to the right and two steps forward... no not there. I didn't give you that ground." No, He says, "I'll give you the land wherever you go."

He gave you His heart, and He promised you His power.

God created you in His image to bear His image in the world. God says, "Listen, I've given you the authority to take steps and I'll give you wherever you step, but you've got to step."

How do we not get out of balance there? I'm just walking around naming and claiming, stepping and grabbing. It's all mine. I have the power. No, he says, "First and foremost, you need to know my heart." How do we know God's heart? He told us everything that is important to Him.

"Then the King will say to those on his right, 'Come, you who are blessed by my Father, inherit the Kingdom prepared for you from the creation of the world. For I was hungry, and you fed me. I was thirsty, and you gave me a drink. I was a stranger, and you invited me into your home. I was naked, and you gave me clothing. I was sick, and you cared for me. I was in prison, and you visited me.'" Matthew 25:34-36

Now, think about that for a second. In the final judgment, when we're standing before God, what matters to God? He tells us right there. "I was hungry and you fed me. I was thirsty and you gave me a drink. I was naked and you clothed me. I was imprisoned and you visited me. I was sick and you cared for me."

"The Spirit of the Lord is upon me, for he has anointed me to bring Good News to the poor. He has sent me to proclaim that captives will be released, that the blind will see, that the oppressed will be set free, and that the time of the Lord's favor has come." Luke 4:18-19

The Spirit of the Lord is upon you for a purpose. If you have God's heart, you can walk in God's power. This might sound strange, but God did not tell us to start a food ministry. We did not have to be told by God.

Does that shock you? He didn't tell us to start a food ministry. In His Word, He has shown us what matters to Him, and because I have God's heart inside of me, He gives me power and I can take a step. Do you know what happens when I take a step? He's going to show up. I don't have to say:

God, I see somebody hungry. What do you want me to do?
God, I see somebody thirsty. What do you want me to do?
I see somebody naked. What do you want me to do?
I wish God would tell me what to do next.

He did. He gave you His heart, and He promised you His power. What do you have to do? You have to push on the gas and steer. "Go. I'll give you every place your foot treads," so don't just stand there still as a stump! Get going!

PUT IT TO WORK

It's hard to believe that we can have the same kind of power that Christ had, but that is exactly what He said! John 14:12, "I tell you the truth, anyone who believes in me will do the same works I have done, and even greater works, because I am going to be with the Father."

Do you believe you can do the same kind of miracles that Jesus did? It's much easier to believe that someone else could... Do you believe YOU can?

When Jesus said we would do miracles, what that means is that you and I, empowered by HIS authority and strength, could look at what seems impossible and make that mountain move by calling on His name in faith! In fact, Jesus said that we would do even greater works than these, it all begins when we're faithful in small things.

What's a small thing you can choose to be faithful in today that God might turn into something miraculous tomorrow?

Jesus fed thousands; working together we can feed tens of thousands.

Epilogue

MORE THAN ENOUGH

When I began writing the sermon series (that became this book), I thought it would never end. I had intended to launch it as a five-week series on small beginnings. One that emphasized the grace of God when we feel we aren't enough. Instead of 5 weeks it ended up at 18 weeks. Now that we have arrived at the end, I hope I've been able to communicate all that God put on my heart, all that He opened in my spirit as I prepared for one Sunday after another. Eighteen weeks is a long time, but I'm not sure I was ready for it to end. There's so much more that God has in store for us when we trust in Him and follow His leading. I pray that you have seen how our God truly is more than Enough. I don't have all the answers, but He does.

He's not an almost enough God. He's not a just enough God. He's a *more than enough* God. If we lean into His More Than Enough presence in our lives, then we can go through hardship, trials, difficulty, and circumstance without losing our hope, joy, and peace. Philippians 4:13 says, *"I can do all things through Christ who strengthens me"* (my favorite misquoted verse ever), the apostle Paul wasn't claiming to be able to leap over tall buildings in a single bound because Jesus was going to give him superhuman strength. In context with the verses that immediately preceded verse 13, Paul was saying (my paraphrase), "I know what it is to be in need, and I know what it is to have plenty. I know what it is to be well fed and what it is to be hungry, I've been a prisoner, and I've been free. Ultimately, this is what I know, I can endure when others would quit. I can be joyful when others lose heart. I can find peace in the middle of the storm because I know who it is who gives me strength."

In our best moments, without God, we find that it is never enough. There will always be a need, something missing. But WITH God we can experience His goodness even when everything seems to be falling apart around us. We've all known people who were doing well. Everything was going their way. Yet they weren't happy or content. Then I've been on the mission field in Uganda where I saw kids who had nearly nothing, who had lost their parents and lived in an orphanage where we were serving. They were laughing and playing between vacation Bible school lessons, cheerfully kicking an empty soda bottle around like a soccer ball. How could that be? Those children knew the love of God the Father. They lived in a home where they were being brought up to know God's goodness, and they had peace. They found that God is enough even when the world around them had been harsh and unkind.

If we truly want Enough of God in our life, we must start by acknowledging that He is all we need.

Here are three ways to experience the sufficiency of God in your life:

HIS WORD

Bury yourself in His Word. Imprint it on your heart. Memorize verses. Don't just go through a routine of reading His Word, though. Before you begin, ask the Holy Spirit to speak to you and lead you as you read. The Bible will give you hope and encourage you in every situation.

THE HOLY SPIRIT

The Holy Spirit lives in you and enables you to stand. He comforts you during the difficult seasons. He encourages you and will guide your steps if you'll learn to follow His gentle leading. God has identified us as His own by placing the Holy Spirit in our hearts as the first installment of everything He has promised us. Pray and ask the Holy Spirit to show you the love of your heavenly Father.

GOD'S PROVIDENCE

Finally, remember that no matter where you are, God will put you in the right place at the right time so you can be a miracle. We need to prepare and be ready for God to use us. God can have us in the right place, locationally and logistically. But if we're not in the right place spiritually to say, "Okay, God, wherever I am at any point in time, I give you permission and freedom to use me wherever you want to use me," then that's a missed opportunity to see God working through us! If we aren't watchful, we can get out of position. *God, keep my heart straight. I've got to believe in your providence because when you set up divine appointments, I must be ready.*

No matter the delay, no matter the missed flight, or being stuck waiting forever on a passing train, count it all joy. You never know what divine appointment you have waiting for you on the other side of the train.

There are hundreds of stories I could tell you to back up everything we have talked about tenfold, and you know I love a good story, but it is time for you to take this journey of Enough and allow God to lead you. Allow Him to use you and allow yourself to be comforted by Him. God is always More Than Enough. Now is the time for you to let Him pour out all He has for you and for you to realize that it truly is . . . Enough.

One final passage that I hope stirs your heart like it stirs mine. The apostle Paul in his second letter to the church in Corinth beginning in chapter 6 (The Message):

"Companions as we are in this work with you, we beg you, please don't squander one bit of this marvelous life God has given us. God reminds us,

I heard your call in the nick of time;

The day you needed me, I was there to help.

Don't put it off; don't frustrate God's work by showing up late, throwing a question mark over everything we're doing. Our work as God's servants gets validated—or not—in the details. People are watching us as we stay at our post, alertly, unswervingly . . . in hard times, tough times, and bad times; when we're beaten up, jailed, and mobbed; working hard, working late, working without eating; with pure heart, clear head, steady hand; in gentleness, holiness, and honest love; when we're telling the truth, and when God's showing his power; when we're doing our best setting things right; when we're praised, and when we're blamed; slandered, and honored; true to our word, though distrusted; ignored by the world, but recognized by God; terrifically alive, though rumored to be dead; beaten within an inch of our lives, but re-

fusing to die; immersed in tears, yet always filled with deep joy; living on handouts, yet enriching many; having nothing, having it all.

Dear, dear Corinthians, I can't tell you how much I long for you to enter this wide-open, spacious life. We didn't fence you in. The smallness you feel comes from within you. Your lives aren't small, but you're living them in a small way. I'm speaking as plainly as I can and with great affection. Open up your lives. Live openly and expansively!"

Don't squander one bit of this marvelous life—this incredible life of chasing after God.

All my love,
Lafe

About the Author

Author, speaker, and pastor Lafe Angell has been serving in ministry most of his life. He graduated from Oral Roberts University in 1993 and, following God's call, became a full-time pastor in 2014. Lafe and his wife, Hope, founded Grace Point Family Church in Anna, Texas, just north of Dallas, in 2020. They launched just seven weeks before the pandemic shutdown and God used what should have killed the church to expand and grow it. Together, Lafe and Hope lead a thriving church that operates a permanent food pantry and sends missionaries around the world. Lafe is a board member for Bring the Light Ministries, a homeless outreach in Dallas.

Lafe and Hope married in July 1995 and have three children together. They live in the Dallas area and love to see God's kingdom advanced and to spread God's grace and mercy wherever they go! If you want to learn more, check out their website www.gracepointfamilychurch.com.